To Loose the Bonds of Injustice

To Loose the Bonds of Injustice

*The Plight of the Mentally Ill
& What the Church Can Do*

Marcia A. Murphy

RESOURCE *Publications* • Eugene, Oregon

TO LOOSE THE BONDS OF INJUSTICE
The Plight of the Mentally Ill & What the Church Can Do

Copyright © 2018 Marcia A. Murphy. All rights reserved. Except for brief quotations in critical publications or reviews, no part of this book may be reproduced in any manner without prior written permission from the publisher. Write: Permissions, Wipf and Stock Publishers, 199 W. 8th Ave., Suite 3, Eugene, OR 97401.

Resource Publications
An Imprint of Wipf and Stock Publishers
199 W. 8th Ave., Suite 3
Eugene, OR 97401

www.wipfandstock.com

PAPERBACK ISBN: 978-1-5326-5385-8
HARDCOVER ISBN: 978-1-5326-5386-5
EBOOK ISBN: 978-1-5326-5387-2

Scripture quotations marked (NRSV) are from the Holy Bible, New Revised Standard Version, copyright © 1989 the Division of Christian Education of the National Council of the Churches of Christ in the United States of America. Used by permission. All rights reserved.

Scripture quotations marked (NIV) are taken from the Holy Bible, New International Version®, NIV®. Copyright © 1973, 1978, 1984, 2011 by Biblica, Inc.™ Used by permission of Zondervan. All rights reserved worldwide. www.zondervan.com The "NIV" and "New International Version" are trademarks registered in the United States Patent and Trademark Office by Biblica, Inc.™

Scripture quotations marked (ESV) are from The Holy Bible, English Standard Version (ESV), copyright ©2001 by Crossway Bibles, a publishing ministry of Good News Publishers. Used by permission. All rights reserved.

Scripture quotations marked (NLT) are taken from the Holy Bible, New Living Translation, copyright ©1996, 2004, 2015 by Tyndale House Foundation. Used by permission of Tyndale House Publishers, Inc., Carol Stream, Illinois 60188. All rights reserved.

Scripture quotations marked (MSG) taken from *THE MESSAGE*. Copyright © by Eugene H. Peterson, 1993, 1994, 1995, 1996. Used by permission of NavPress Publishing Group.

Scripture quotations marked (KJV) are taken from the King James Version, published in 1611. The King James Version of the Bible is in the public domain.

Thank you for the permission granted to reprint portions from the following work:

"Standing in the Breach," (sermon) by R. Charles Grant, DMin, Bon Air Presbyterian Church, Virginia. Reproduced by permission of R. Charles Grant, DMin.

Building Moral Intelligence: the seven essential virtues that teach kids to do the right thing by Michele Borba, EdD, Copyright © 2001. Reproduced by permission of Michele Borba, EdD.

Out of Sight, Out of Mind by Frank L. Wright Jr., Copyright © 1945, National Mental Health Association, Disability History Museum. Courtesy of Swarthmore College Peace Collection. (http://www.disabilitymuseum.org/dhm/lib/detail.html?id=1754&page=all)

Manufactured in the U.S.A.

To some whom I have witnessed, with great courage and sacrifice, have been *standing in the breach:* Russell Noyes Jr., MD (Lutheran), Del Miller, MD, PharmD (Mennonite), Scott Temple, PhD (Jewish), Scott Grau, PhD (Jewish), Timothy H. Little, DMin, (Presbyterian), Phillip Cary, PhD (Episcopalian), Fr. Jeff Belger, MDiv (Roman Catholic), and Daniel R. Stout, MA (Lutheran).

May their labors be not in vain. . . .

"Is not this the fast that I choose:
to loose the bonds of injustice,
to undo the thongs of the yoke,
to let the oppressed go free,
and to break every yoke?
Is it not to share your bread with the hungry,
and bring the homeless poor into your house;
when you see the naked, to cover them,
and not to hide yourself from your own kin? . . .
If you remove the yoke from among you,
the pointing of the finger, the speaking of evil,
if you offer your food to the hungry
and satisfy the needs of the afflicted,
then your light shall rise in the darkness
and your gloom be like the noonday . . .
Your ancient ruins shall be rebuilt;
you shall raise up the foundations of many generations;
you shall be called *the repairer of the breach*,
the restorer of streets to live in."

ISAIAH 58:6–7, 9B–10, 12 (NRSV)

Contents

Acknowledgments | xi
Author's Note | xii
Introduction | xiii

1. Turning a Deaf Ear | 1
2. Challenges and Reforms | 23
3. Civility, Grace, and Mental Health | 45
4. Cultural Expectations and Christian Identity | 73
5. He Stretched Out His Hand and Touched Him | 93

Bibliography | 121

Acknowledgments

THE INDIVIDUALS OF THE Prayer Ministry of St. Andrew Presbyterian Church have been an invaluable part of my life with their generous support of my ministry work and programs over the years. The great compassion and power of this vital group of diverse men and women that has lifted up my work, and sometimes my personal health, for God's blessing and fruitfulness has been a dynamic force without which I never would have made it. Without their persistent, loving prayers I could not have done as much or been as effective. I am constantly reminded of how sacrificial and supportive this group has been and continues to be; I owe them a big thank you.

I also wish to express my gratitude to Jeff Charis-Carlson and Myrna Farraj for their excellent editorial suggestions. Thank you for all you've done to assist me in this work.

Author's Note

THIS IS A WORK of nonfiction; however, in order to protect the privacy of individuals involved some names, characteristics, and locations have been altered. The exceptions are names of prominent figures and institutions which are known to the public.

Introduction

I AM A CHRISTIAN who has lived the life of a mental patient in the United States during the period between the closures of the big institutions in the 1950s and the advent of community care-based treatments. My new book, *To Loose the Bonds of Injustice*, is an inside view of the deplorable conditions faced by people who experience mental illness and the vital role the church and society must play to counteract those conditions.

This book builds upon the insights provided in my earlier memoir, *Voices in the Rain: Meaning in Psychosis*, in which I shared my story of what it was like to have a psychosis, post-traumatic stress disorder, and clinical depression. I described my experience with mental illness through which I found spiritual meaning and, ultimately, God. Please refer back to *Voices in the Rain* for information on my experience of psychiatric disability and the importance of religious faith in the recovery process.

As I am in a stable condition it would be very easy to simply sit back and relax, letting the box fan cool me in a luxurious indifference as I sip my iced tea, blocking out from my memory the drama of my adult life as well as how it is for the vast majority of people with psychiatric disabilities, many of whom are struggling to survive and are on the streets.

To Loose the Bonds of Injustice is my initiative to inform and educate others about social justice issues of mental health. I share my experiences, reflections, observations and interpretations. Instead of an academic look from the outside, this is an inside view of

Introduction

someone who has a lot to say about the issues that prevent people who have a mental illness from living full and productive lives.

Efforts at reform go back several centuries. In the 1800's Dorothea Dix led a movement to release mentally ill people unjustly held in jails and alms houses or who were homeless, and instigated the building of large mental institutions.[1] These institutions, however, only resulted in warehousing the ill under deplorable conditions without any treatments provided—largely, because no treatments were available.

Conditions worsened over the next half century, even as conscientious objectors were given the opportunity during the world wars to work in mental institutions rather than be deployed for combat. One such objector, Frank L. Wright, Jr., provided eye witness accounts of the deprivation and suffering within institutional walls:

> In my heart were thousands of mental patients and their families, many of whom I had come to know personally, whose anguish and bafflement knew no bounds. And in my mind were the millions of Americans who know so little, and therefore care so little, about those forgotten thousands who are in our mental hospitals.[2]

Such inhumane conditions, combined with doctors who thought the patients as less than human, led to the point that they created barbaric procedures to remove the frontal lobes of their patients' brains. The procedures—graphically depicted in the 2008 film, *The Lobotomist*—were performed in at least fifty state asylums often without patients' consent or foreknowledge. The results were devastating. Such abuse was legitimized by the medical industry, championed by Walter Freeman, a neurologist, until it became public knowledge and an outcry against it halted such

---

1. Gollaher, *Voice for the Mad*, 6.
2. Wright Jr., *Out of Sight, Out of Mind*, Preface, para. 1.

INTRODUCTION

actions. Freeman was "decried a moral monster"[3] and "lobotomy, one of the most barbaric mistakes of modern medicine."[4]

While Freedman and his colleagues were engaged in "one of the darkest chapters in psychiatric history,"[5] others were building more humane academic treatment centers, seeking solutions based on healing and compassionate care. University hospitals constructed adjacent facilities with the focus on psychiatric illness and research from a scientific perspective. And from these academic professionals, a new mindset emerged to eliminate stigma and to provide solutions that could improve the quality of life for the mentally ill. In addition, the field of Social Work partnered with psychiatry, becoming a powerful force in advancing this cause.

By the twenty-first century, facilities in the state of Iowa like the Independence Mental Health Institute and the Mt. Pleasant Mental Health Institute, had largely become museum-like buildings, functional only to treat a few dozen patients after decades of holding hundreds. Within the next decade, Iowa's governor closed them down, gutted the state's county-based mental health system and cut off support for thousands of people with mental illness. The results are not surprising: the suicide rate keeps going up. Opioid abuse is epidemic. Anger erupts into violence across our headlines.

I have witnessed first-hand the effects of these state-wide budget cuts to mental health services and I describe the devastating conditions of what is left in place to care for those with mental illness. I discuss some of the societal roots of discrimination and attitudes of neglect which leave vulnerable people out in the cold, both figuratively and literally.

In *To Loose the Bonds of Injustice*, I applaud the heroic attempts of psychiatry in the West, healthcare providers who struggle to meet the demand in their clinics due to lack of funding to support them. I describe how subsequently and reluctantly, many

3. Goodman, The Lobotomist, *PBS Home Video*.
4. Ibid.
5. Ibid.

of the mentally ill are turned away because of the lack of available psychiatric staff and/or hospital beds. Although most of my specific examples come from Iowa, treatments are deficient on a national and global scale. My assessment of such shortage leads to recommendations for how to implement needed changes.

In *To Loose the Bonds of Injustice*, I share thoughts on the activities I found meaningful within the church and in the broader community often while encountering strong prejudices and barriers. Struggling to get my basic needs met is a reoccurring theme: a life of poverty at a subsistence level; disincentives for employment and discrimination; scarcity of affordable housing and the threat of homelessness; societal rejection (exclusion) and subsequent isolation; difficulties with groups; learning new social skills and values that help to halt the cycle of abuse learned while growing up. I explain how it is nearly impossible to survive without a caring community of faith. This material delves into widespread conditions that hinder recovery. I describe how poverty has affected so many with mental illness and how material deprivation and emotional devastation go hand in hand. Such multifaceted challenges reveal the importance of religious faith and supportive religious and civic communities.

The major theme emerging from all this is the question of meaning: meaning found in my suffering, meaning found in spirituality, and meaning in the religious paradigm inherent in my story. This work will go into depth exploring issues which concern the mentally ill on physical, emotional, and spiritual levels. How can we, the mentally ill, understand our suffering? How does a person with mental illness find hope in the face of adversity? When everything seems pointless and full of dead ends, how does a person pick himself up and go forward?

Religious faith is of paramount importance for those who struggle with mental illness. The role of personal faith and religious communities play a vital role in social integration, healing of the person, and renewal. Those with mental illness and care providers—medical, religious, or familial—may find this information

Introduction

helpful in regard to how to interpret mental health issues and extreme suffering in light of religious faith.

Another theme that emerges is: Human interaction, verbal and behavioral, as an often neglected factor in the epidemiology of psychiatric disorders in this age of pharmaceutical interventions. I suggest that there is a strong connection between social environments and mental health outcomes.

Although it may seem obvious, many people need to be reminded repeatedly of a few basic points: Those who suffer from mental illnesses are *human beings*—born from a mother, were usually brought up in a family, went to school, and interacted with the outer culture.

Second, people with mental illness *can experience pain*. They have feelings that can get hurt. They are not immune from suffering. They also get hungry and thirsty so they need food and drink. They need clothes to wear and shelter to protect them from the elements.

Third, people with mental illness *need to love and to be loved*: they need warm, caring relationships in the form of friendships. They need to be treated with the same dignity that any other member of the human race deserves regardless of ability, socioeconomic status, race, ethnicity, or gender.

Over the course of my adult life I have struggled to obtain food, clothing, and shelter. Why didn't I just find a job? I tried. At last count, I had worked in twenty paid employment positions. I had only completed one year of college, however, so I could only find entry level jobs with low pay. In addition, for many years my emotional stability was nil, having been ostracized by those whom society deem "normal." As a result, I did not have a sufficient social network to support me emotionally. I often went to work when I was hungry and did not have appropriate work clothes. I remember once I wore my deceased grandmother's housedress to my job at Sears. It was one she had worn when doing her cleaning and cooking.

Where was the church in all of this? I tried to attend various congregations, but lacked transportation.

Introduction

Where was my family in all of this? Periodically there was support, but there were also times when I was largely abandoned. My former psychiatrist wrote in my medical record: "Neglect from Marcia's relatives is severe." Once in a while I got some partial help, but it was not sustained on a consistent level throughout my life, and then I was left to flounder by myself.

How could I buy underwear when I couldn't afford it? How could I get a winter coat? Forget about boots! I would make frequent trips to a Crisis Center food pantry where, sometimes, all that was left when I got through the line was bread, canned beans, and bottles of green salad dressing with expired dates.

But I was in good company. I soon realized that the whole mass of humanity was apparently suffering too and I did not have a corner on the market. Now I have reached the point where I'd like to tell about things that cause problems for those with psychiatric disabilities and to offer insights in an effort to improve their lives.

How do we, the mentally ill, find ourselves in this position? Why are we in this situation? In *To Loose the Bonds of Injustice* I look at many factors: personal choices; familial, workplace, organizational environments; benefit programs and society in general. I examine the different facets of the cultural milieu and briefly touch on how non-Western cultures differ in their care and treatment of the ill. What can we learn from one another and how are personal identities formed? I discuss the role of psychiatry and community-based care within a model that would address typical concerns of the mentally ill based on my own experience. The limits which have been imposed upon psychiatry in modern times are significant for those who have been denied treatment due to insufficient funding for clinics and community services.

The point of this project is this: When it comes to mental health and mental disability what do we as individual members of a community value in life and how do our society's priorities mirror these choices? I believe that when whole segments of society take part in denying a certain group the same compassion, understanding, and support that would be given to others, then a barrier is put into place that denies the right to life for this devalued group. The

INTRODUCTION

powerful, in proclaiming that some are not worthy of life by cutting funds and other resources necessary for survival, are putting themselves into the position of God, deciding who shall live and who shall die. Only when the tables are turned and a powerful person might fall victim to an accident that disables, or he or she has an unplanned illness, or becomes elderly with the limits that aging brings, will they see themselves in the same position as the weak. And then who will grant *them* the compassion, understanding, and support that they, themselves, have denied to others?

The Church, those who follow Christ, can bring desperately needed hope to the afflicted. The Bible clearly portrays a God who cares about those with disabilities, many of whom have been discarded by the wider culture.

I share my experiences, thoughts and reflections with the intent to make a difference, stating my view of what positive changes need to be implemented on three levels: individual, organizational and societal level. I describe how vitally important it is for religious organizations to move toward inclusion of those who struggle, welcoming them into their communities, embracing them as children of God. With the enactment of social integration there is a possibility of a better quality of life for all involved—for all individuals have gifts to help build up the church, even *the least of these*....

Organizations are made up of individuals, many of whom belong to religious communities. These same people decide on social policy, rules and regulations. When the church teaches its congregants to compassionately love, forgive, and support people with mental health challenges, this will systemically branch out into the greater community. In this effort, I provide a model of care that has been proven to be successful based on my own personal experience and which is applicable for future community program planning.

My book stresses the importance of education as a key to bringing change to the world with the Church spearheading the movement that restores the dignity and human rights of the mentally ill poor. I explore interconnecting topics on multiple levels

INTRODUCTION

in ways that have not yet been approached in other literature. It is for those who know of someone suffering with a mental illness as well as the general public; the ill themselves, relatives, health care providers, educators, those in religious organizations, and government officials. With this offer of in-depth insights an invitation is extended to the reader to examine habits of the heart. From out of indifference and complacency let there be a growing compassion and an emergence of actions–steps going forward to improve the quality of life for and with all those with mental health needs.

Chapter 1

Turning a Deaf Ear

> Our courts oppose the righteous, / and justice
> is nowhere to be found.
>
> Truth stumbles in the streets, / and honesty
> has been outlawed.
>
> Yes, truth is gone, / and anyone who renounces
> evil is attacked.
>
> The Lord looked and was displeased / to find
> there was no justice.
>
> He was amazed to see that no one intervened /
> to help the oppressed.
>
> So he himself stepped in to save them with
> his strong arm,
>
> and his justice sustained him.
>
> He put on righteousness as his body armor
> and placed the helmet of salvation on his head.
>
> He clothed himself with a robe of vengeance
> and wrapped himself in a cloak of divine passion.
>
> Isaiah 59:14-17 (NLT)

To Loose the Bonds of Injustice

One Christmas a friend of mine gave me a camera and a few weeks later drove me to the Johnson County Poor Farm so I could see and document first-hand what conditions were like for those who could not make it on their own some 150 years ago. My ongoing project represented the assertion of human dignity for all mentally ill persons.

> The 1855 Johnson County Historic Poor Farm, is a window on nineteenth century definitions and policy dealing with perceived social problems. The need to care for the poor or mentally ill had been established in the United States in the 1820s as a duty of the state and local governments. This duty was recognized early in Johnson County history. The County chose first to contract care usually from local physicians. In 1855, the Johnson County supervisors decided to procure 160 acres on the edge of Iowa City for a "poor farm" to provide systematic care with economy . . . and a few hundred feet to the east is the county's most recent facility, Chatham Oakes built in 1964 (now privatized).[1]

The tour guide unlocked the doors of the insane asylum wing that was constructed on the Poor Farm in 1859 and was used until 1886. It is a small building recently painted white. The early reformers, most likely solid Christian people, had good intentions, seeking a solution to the homeless insane who undoubtedly wandered the streets. Sometimes the mentally ill left their abusive homes or were rejected by relatives because of difficult behavior problems. They were unsightly, unkempt, with straggly hair and unbathed. Often, because of starvation, they took food as they walked through the markets without paying for the items. This landed them in jail, a place without adequate provisions which were rat-infested shacks with no legal recourse.

From the time of the Declaration of Independence (1776) and on into the early nineteenth century, counties did what they called "leasing out" but was, in reality, the selling of the mentally ill

---

1. Johnson County Historical Society, "Johnson County Historic Poor Farm," lines 1–7, 24–25.

Turning a Deaf Ear

and poor. Bids were made on each individual and the lowest offer won out. Picture if you can a slave auction where the person being auctioned stands on a platform in front of a group. The person succeeding in the lowest bid then acquires all legal rights over the slave who is stripped of all rights and freedoms. The slave owner can demand any kind of labor and the person with mental illness is forced to work without pay.[2] What may have prevented the continuance of this government-sanctioned selling of human beings was the action of Congress on January 31, 1865, the passing and ratification on December 6, 1865, of the 13th amendment which abolished slavery in the United States and provides that "Neither slavery nor involuntary servitude, except as a punishment for crime whereof the party shall have been duly convicted, shall exist within the United States, or any place subject to their jurisdiction."[3] Even though abolished by law, this slave trade continued well into the twentieth century in some southern states.[4]

Throughout the centuries, the mentally ill have been looked down on and their situation considered beyond hope. Families usually rejected the ill family member; and if a female who was mentally ill did not have a male provider—a husband or father—to look out for her welfare and she was too ill to teach in the town's schools, she ended up homeless. On the streets she would be taken advantage of, sexually abused, a victim of violence and starvation. City officials, if they took notice, would place her under the care of a physician, paying the physician a small fee. The mentally ill male was not much better off. If he had anger or aggression issues and no one could control him, he was locked up, most likely in the county jail. The early reformers were trying to create a space for the mentally ill that would be a step above the jails; however, the asylum wing at the poor farm had too much in common with the jail. As in our modern times, economics was an issue for how well structures could be built or if they could be built at all. Would taxes have to be increased and an allotment funneled into this project?

2. Pietikainen, *Madness*, 92–93.
3. National Archives, "Thirteenth Amendment," lines 2–5.
4. Pietikainen, *Madness*, 92–3.

If so, how would citizens react to the increase? Revolt was always a possibility. City officials risked losing their jobs. At any rate, the asylum was constructed with hope of getting the mentally ill off the streets and out of an over-crowded jail, possibly, as the old adage goes: "out of sight, out of mind."

I found a good description of this asylum in a search at the State Historical Society online. Previously, I had visited a branch of this institution in Iowa City for my research and found a lot of helpful information regarding this particular part of our Iowa history.

> The structure is 24 feet wide and 50 feet long. The eight-bay side elevations have rectangular windows. Vertical wood siding reaches from ground level to the sills. Above, the siding is horizontal. The roof is covered with sheet metal (a later 1900s addition). There is no foundation beneath the structure. Flooring is of wide, rough planks, many of which have been broken or removed. Walls and ceiling are also planked. The interior contains a central hall running the full length of the building. Off it on each side are cells, approximately 7'x7', with horizontal plank walls and vertical 2"x4"s used to create the barred front of each. Each cell had a door, also of 2"x4"s, and a few retain their iron fastenings. Beside each door is a narrow, horizontal opening through which inmates were given food. Treatment was nonexistent, heat provided only by a small stove in the hallway, and the amount of physical care administered here was probably little more than that given the hogs who occupied the structure in later years beginning in 1886.[5]

With some trepidation I entered and saw that the structure was in a deteriorated condition including some of the window glass, gone. I felt intuitively as though the whole wing had been full of human misery. With pain I imagined desperate people confined, dressed in rags and existing under unsanitary inhumane

---

5. Miltner, Mr. and Mrs. Joe, "First Johnson County Asylum," lines 6–7, 10–16, 37–40.

Turning a Deaf Ear

conditions. Although now swept clean, I felt certain that back then dirt and litter covered the floors of the cells.

The single pot-bellied stove which still stands in the center of the hallway is reminiscent of an insufficient heat source during Midwestern frigid winters. To give you some idea of how severe the conditions were for those in the asylum, this is how bad it gets in Iowa: not far away, Elkader, Iowa, roughly 100 miles north of Johnson County, has the record for the lowest temperatures in the state.

> On February 3, 1996, Elkader, Iowa, fell to -43.9 degrees Celsius (-47 Fahrenheit). Polar bears can survive that kind of frigid weather, but humans cannot without protection. Thermometer readings that low may be rare, but Iowa has a history of producing sub-zero temperatures year after year.[6]

By sight and feel I could tell that the walls of the asylum were made of incredibly thin wooden boards, so thin, any extreme cold would have easily penetrated and the inmates would have painfully frozen, some, I'm sure, to their deaths.

But have conditions improved for people who have a mental illness? Let me fast-forward to that previously cited record-low February day in 1996. Where was I? And what was I doing then?

Not far down the road from that county farm and asylum, only two and a half miles east to be exact, I struggled to keep warm. At that time I was able to rent an apartment in a complex probably built in the 1940s, a multi-storied brick building that had hot water plumbing for the heat source. A giant boiler for the entire building was in the basement. However, when I moved in, I didn't know that my unit's heating system, which included pipes that lined the walls, was broken. As time went on and the December cold turned into frigid January and February, I struggled to keep warm.

My apartment was in the northwest corner of the middle floor of the building and, in addition, was on a somewhat open west side of town where wind was a constant factor. I tried to keep out

---

6. Lee, *Iowa's Winter Cold Temperature History*, lines 1–4.

the cold wind by taping up plastic sheeting around the large living room picture window and bedroom windows. I wore extra clothing but it was still cold. In desperation, I did some things I now know are dangerous: I turned on my gas stove for heat and left the door open. I climbed into bed with additional blankets with a floor space heater turned on high. To make matters worse there was the added factor of snowfall as the wind whipped through the walls. Even my cat felt like he was freezing. We suffered together.

A few years later I was able to move to a different building across the courtyard in the complex. Surely, things would improve. Then, winter time came and, oh my goodness! The building's boiler broke down. It was, again, below zero outside and now I was, again, without a heat source. My only family nearby was an inhospitable relative who had a history of violent aggression against me—having threatened my life at one time. Where I was attending church, I had not met many people so that didn't seem to be a source for help. I had been friends with a man for seven years who owned his own duplex, living on one side and renting out the other. He said he would help.

My friend let me stay at his place for several days as my landlord dealt with the replacing the building's boiler while the temperature in my apartment fell below freezing (it was below zero outside). He, very properly, slept on the couch, and I was in another room. This was life-saving. I can now only imagine the extreme suffering for those poor mental patients back in the asylum in the 1800s who had insufficient clothing and only thin wooden walls between them and the extreme cold. I can even see myself among them, shivering and huddled in a corner of my cell for the slightest bit of extra warmth, and wondering why God would allow anyone to be born into a world that treats them so cruelly.

* * *

Of major importance for people with mental illness is how the scientific community views the cause of mental illness and disability. The emergence of new theories in the field of genetics have a profound impact upon funding, therapeutic treatments, and, subsequently, recovery outcomes for the disabled. However, a leading psychiatric researcher at the University of Iowa informed me that currently there are no findings that have been consistently replicated showing scientific evidence of a genetic link to any of the mental illnesses.

An important book on this subject that touches upon, among other things, the topic of genetic research is Hans Reinders's *The Future of the Disabled in Liberal Society*.[7] Reinders is concerned about genetic research with the ethical implications for the disabled. For example, how and why are disabled people discriminated against? What are the implications for their lives resulting from genetic counseling and prejudicial treatment?[8]

I need to point out that all of us are what we call "temporarily-abled." As we age many things happen to our bodies that in one way or another will disable us either partially or totally. We are also only one car accident away from being disabled ourselves, so these issues are relevant to everyone.

Were the people who were held behind bars against their will, in the nineteenth century asylum treated any better than those euthanized by German Nazis in their Aktion T-4 program? I can imagine that the people held as prisoners in poor farm asylum experienced a living death. The Judeo-Christian religion, the religious tradition I was brought up in, supports the notion of compassion for the weak and sick and, in modern-day America, there are some people, such as many in the health care industry, who uphold a type of "dignity of life" philosophy for human beings. However, had I lived in Nazi Germany from 1939 into the mid-1940s, my life would most likely have been cut short. It would have been ended by the Nazi regime who would have labeled me a "useless eater."[9]

What began with the eugenics movement in the United States in the early 1900s, a movement to cosmetically harness the reproduction of human beings with the aim of creating the best genetic

7. Reinders, *The Future of the Disabled*, ix, 1–9.
8. Ibid.,
9. Mostert, "Useless Eaters," 155.

outcome, turned into a mindset that soon made its way across the ocean to Germany. There eugenics was adopted in the attempt to cleanse the German society of the weak or the undesirables: those considered to be "inferior," those who had a physical, emotional or mental disability or were elderly, along with homosexuals, gypsies, and Jews. In order to establish the "superior race," the Nazis murdered thousands of disabled babies, children, adults and elderly by lethal injection, gassing, or starvation.[10]

I share this history because one would wonder what kind of society could commit such heinous acts. When we look at eugenics and people with disabilities, who can decide who is worthy of care, or life or death? How do we judge a human being's worth? How do we treat those that society sees as weak and dependent? What are the attitudes and values of a people who would allow and even aggressively pursue extermination of the most weak and vulnerable of its citizens? The depravity knew no bounds. Few had the courage to resist but some members of the Roman Catholic Church protested, risking their lives.[11]

Though reformers with good intensions have periodically instigated change over the centuries, there is still a long history of societal neglect, mistreatment, and indifference on the part of our Western culture concerning the plight of the mentally ill. Change usually comes with two steps forward and then two or three steps back. Beginning in 1843, Dorothea Dix pushed for reform by persuading state and federal bodies to fund the construction of large institutions all across the entire country.[12] As a result, thousands of people were warehoused and cut off from society, inadequately cared for with virtually no treatment because no treatments were available. I can image how they felt: formerly mistreated in jails and alms houses, only to be forced into large prison-like institutions, freedoms denied, abandoned, and left to die.

* * *

10. Ibid.
11. Ibid., 165.
12. Gollaher, *Voice for the Mad*, 6.

Turning a Deaf Ear

On September 16, 2011, a married couple from church who are friends of mine, drove me to the Mental Health Institute in Mount Pleasant, a small city in southeast Iowa. It was a cold, rainy day, rather dark and dreary. The trip took about ninety minutes until we turned into a long drive-way, then pulled into a parking lot on the west side of a large structure. Built in 1855, parts of the weather-worn, gray, stone building had a look and feel of an old historical period that sharply contrasts with our modern day twenty-first century facilities.

Directly next door on the left was a huge multi-story modern 600-unit men's prison encircled with a big metal fence with barbed wire on the top. A women's prison was on the right, consisting of a smaller separate building. Based on the notion that prisoners and mental patients should be separated, the state of Iowa did the "flip-flop" in 1981, dramatically increasing the number of prison units in contrast to a major decrease in psychiatric facility beds. The result was a catastrophic lessening in treatment options for those with mental illness and those with behavioral issues secondary to mental illness. Most prisons provide few treatments or next to nothing in terms of psychiatric care.

Our tour guide gave us a block of time for the entire morning. Even though this facility originally had a several-hundred-bed capacity, it now only had nine beds for the psychiatric unit and about forty-five for dual diagnosis and substance abuse residential treatment. First, we were shown rooms where the patients sleep and then a day room with chairs and sofas where a small group of female residents in dual diagnosis were viewing a movie on a big screen TV. One of the women looked over at me from across the room and smiled. She looked pleasant. We saw a bathroom with a single tub and a giant container of shampoo which led me to think that the women have to wait a long time for a bath. We met some of the staff—nurses' aides, counselors, and a social worker—who seemed very caring. Our tour guide emphasized that he hoped for psychiatric care to return to being nurturing, loving, and kind.

We saw the former dusty medical records room that had several shelves holding huge journal type books no longer in use.

Our guide took one record book down and opened it for us. It had records on some of the first patients dating back to 1861. I was struck by how beautiful and elegant the handwriting was but was unable to make out what it said. Our guide said the administration was working on finding a new home for them where they would be safe from fire, and preserved, safe and protected as in a museum or the state historical society.

Our guide took us to the facility's old morgue, also no longer in use. He explained that the deceased patients' bodies would be kept in rectangular box containers. The room's contents had only been emptied in recent months.

We then visited the cafeteria in the basement which was still functional. This large room was an eerie, dimly lit area with a front area where the patients would be served cafeteria-style as they carried trays down a line. The large room had a low ceiling with visible plumbing. The walls and items in the room were of a dingy, dark greenish-gray color including a dozen extremely old and well-used tables and chairs. The linoleum squared floors had permanent black dirt stuck in noticeable cracks and tears. We were later told that the staff had sent out requests for the funding of new tables and chairs that could be bolted to the floor. Our guide stated that there were times when patients would violently hit people with the furniture, throwing it around the room at one another and staff. Many people had become injured, some quite seriously. It seemed like a very sad, dark room. At the time of our tour, there were two prisoners eating. They were men who were assigned chores in the mental health facility as part of their sentence. There was also a little side room used as a kitchen which had a refrigerator and cupboards. What struck me most about the dining area was that it scared me. It was so very gloomy and my friends later agreed with me that it seemed rather frightening, with a heavy historical atmosphere of extreme human emotions such as violence, fear, and hopelessness.

We saw the art therapy room which had lots of materials on tables and art work hanging. Our tour guide told us that the art director takes the materials to the units and the patients create things there. Our guide said he had a lot of respect for the work this employee does.

The guide showed us the laundry room which had a large number of stacked navy blue sweat pants. I asked the aide if they give them out for the patients to use and take home. He answered that they wash them and use them over and over again.

The guide took us inside the institute's library, which was a tranquil and pleasant room, very spacious, clean and neat, containing shelves of books and magazines with several tables and chairs. I noticed the floor was carpeted. At the side was a locked door where the staff kept the movies and professional journals. At the hour we were there, it was not being used, but I was sure that at other times of the day it must have been a peaceful, quiet place for the patients. The guide said there were educational classes offered for the patients like anger management and self-esteem. The patients have structure all day long with various activities. Our guide told us that a pastor leads a worship service every Sunday and there is a Bible study every Friday. The guide said that he believed religious faith was a very important part of the patients' lives.

We went to the gym, and the guide said it was a "God-send." They used it a lot. The patients played basketball and used exercise machines. He then showed us the back yard that had a picnic table shelter and a tennis court. This was a big grassy area with lots of trees which looked beautiful. Back inside, he took us to a rotunda with meeting rooms and large windows. In the institute's hallways along the walls were many photos and framed news clippings depicting the past history of the institute, some describing a disastrous fire in in the building in 1936.

Toward the end of the tour the guide told us that the institute's budget was very tight, there were problems trying to get all the psychiatric care funded. There were restrictions and red tape. It was a constant challenge to come up with enough money. He said they had to do more and more things but with much less money and less staff. They had a problem with burn out and not being able to take vacations. The guide said that when he had to have surgery on his knee and was recuperating in his home, he had to take phone calls from institute staff and answer questions regarding work. He was not able to separate work from home life and at one time went through a depression, relying heavily on his supportive wife who helped him recover.

My general impression when we left was that the institute has been a place of great suffering, not only for the patients, but also for the staff. The dimly lit hallways and rooms mirror the hopelessness of the souls who stayed there. Heroic staff, determined against all odds to help and to heal, must not be forgotten or underappreciated. They were determined to help the patients with what little resources they had. Our guide was very gracious and generous with his time and additional materials he provided.

The Iowa governor closed the Mount Pleasant Mental Health Institute and another facility in western Iowa, the Clarinda Mental Health Institute, in 2015, adding to the severe bed shortage already in the state. The closure earned Iowa the lowest ranking for available psychiatric beds in the country: last place.

* * *

I am of the opinion that the amount of services for the mentally ill throughout history and what currently is available is a reflection upon the societal values and, subsequently, attitudes towards those who have a psychiatric illness or disability. In biblical times, it was the leper who was the outcast. And now in modern times, it has been my experience that the mentally ill are, to many, the "undesirables" of our Western culture. To suffer from this disability, as I do, one is placed at the mercy of the able-bodied and strong-minded.

In 2012, I asked an expert in the field of psychiatry about the urgent need for more community centers and hospital services to care for and treat people with mental illness. I asked if the biggest obstacle in mental health care is the inaccessibility of the system for the majority of the mentally ill. The professor replied: "I'm not sure if it is the majority—but it is a large number and a very real and extremely important issue."[13]

---

13. Psychiatric professional, email message to author, January 4, 2012.

Turning a Deaf Ear

It seems to be largely economics. When the state or county has fiscal problems they think of what programs they can cut. More often than not it will be the social programs that are reduced or axed because the constituents who make up the segment of the society who benefit from them, the sick, disabled, and poor, cannot financially contribute to a politician's fund raising efforts; plus, they may be less likely to vote in elections. But of course since the wealthy can and often do—the policies and regulations favor the well off—systematically oppressing humanitarian movements to improve the living standards and quality of life for the marginalized.

Every once in a while defenders of the powerless take the reins; but these occurrences are few and far between. Meanwhile, city officials may attempt to build recreational facilities or will allow luxury real estate dwellings on land where low-rent housing should be developed; thus, homeless population increases.

The medical industry has a long and complex history of both helping and harming those who are vulnerable. Every institution will have kind-hearted as well as hard-hearted individuals reflecting diverse philosophical leanings towards patient care. In the extreme form, the weak and vulnerable have even been eliminated. The question of what makes a life worthwhile is quietly debated in board rooms where budgets are determined.

So how do we currently stand in the early twenty-first century? The care and treatment of the mentally ill in the United States has reached a new low, previously only matched in the nineteenth century when the majority of those with mental illness, along with the poor and disabled, were largely confined to jails right along with those convicted of crimes or were left homeless on the streets. Even though it's common knowledge among legislative bodies that therapeutic intervention and housing within the community is highly cost effective and cheaper than jail time, many short-sighted and callous law makers turn their backs on the experts' recommendations. The common sense of supporting the mentally ill in rehabilitation programs is rejected in favor of locking people up behind bars where medication and therapy is often denied.

As Terry Rickers, then a district court judge in Iowa's fifth judicial district, noted in 2011:

> Iowa's mental health system must be reformed... Warehousing mentally ill patients in jails and prisons that are not equipped to treat them is unacceptable. Our society is better than that. More efficiency is necessary, but it is wrong to believe we can solve mental health issues without dedication of sufficient monetary and human capital. We can no longer afford to ignore the problems with Iowa's mental health system.[14]

Not only did things not improve for the better since then; things got progressively worse. In January 2012, I went to the Statehouse in Des Moines, Iowa. After months of preparation, on the first day of the new session, I ensured a packet of materials was placed on every legislator's desk. In the packet, I encouraged lawmakers to provide more funding and services for the mentally ill in our state. Experts in the field had signed my document, providing endorsements.

I talked with Stephen Trefz, LISW, Special Projects Director, at the Abbe Center for Community Health in Iowa City. He made the following comments:

> In any one year, 25% of the population may be diagnosed with a mental disorder. Out of that number, historically 40% seek treatment. So I would speculate that not a majority of Iowans with a mental illness diagnosis are being treated, especially when you account for the uninsured Iowans who cannot afford treatment.[15]

As I mentioned earlier, Iowa Gov. Terry Branstad proceeded to close some of the state mental institutions, just leaving two open—both with reduced beds. He also cut nursing staff in long-term care facilities to dangerously low levels that left both patients and staff in unsafe conditions. Most of the local hospitals across

---

14. Rickers, "Mental Health in Iowa: Lack of facilities," Des Moines Register, 6 OP.
15. Trefz, email message to author, April 3, 2012.

the state closed their psychiatric units; only a few remained. The state's sole tertiary care facility remained and subsequently became overloaded with patients seeking care from not only around the state, but from the greater region. The law makers did not seem to understand the problem or the consequences of not funding such facilities.

Here are a healthcare provider's words on the situation for the psychiatric out-patient clinics at Iowa's sole tertiary state hospital:

> The system is so back-logged that the patients often cannot get in for treatment in a timely fashion. Many of these people end up falling through the cracks and end up back in the ER or hospital. We see this happening all the time.[16]

One hundred percent of admissions to the state tertiary care center psychiatric in-patient units are patients in an acute crisis situation, people who are considered a danger to themselves or to others. It is unfortunate that only these extreme cases can be hospitalized. There are many others who need critical care who cannot be admitted.

There is, of course, a segment of the mentally ill population that has received help with medical care, disability financial supports, housing, and who are provided with bare necessities. Some are aided by sympathetic relatives, with others given shelter under a paid professional's wing who went to bat for the patient to obtain benefits when they were too ill to help themselves. Whatever the method of support provided, it is the undergirding value of compassion that is upholding and safeguarding the ill so they will not perish from a lack of resources.

* * *

For the mentally ill person living in poverty there are many obstacles to independence. *Can you imagine residing in the United States and living on $9,060 a year? Or $755 a month?* After you catch your breath, it becomes clear why federal housing assistance programs

16. Psychiatric professional, email message to author, January 4, 2012.

are important which aid with rent—apartments costing $545 (usually more) rent a month; and why the food stamps aid is necessary even when the portions allotted are meager. Anything helps a person struggling at the poverty or sub-poverty levels.

The mentally ill in Western culture are being punished for being ill and are put in what feels like economic jail, though we are free to walk away from it at any given time to live homeless on the streets. The mentally ill have initially committed no crime yet are treated as people who've insulted the common good. The mentally ill are provided supports such as Supplemental Security Income (SSI), Social Security Disability Income (SSDI), Medicaid, Medicare, and as I mentioned, housing assistance, and food stamps. But these are all provided at such a minimal level that it is not enough to sustain life. Then if one tries to get a job to improve one's situation without a college degree or if a diagnosis is revealed, one can only get the entry level bottom jobs which will not pay the rent and supply all the basic survival needs. Having a diagnosis of one of the mental illnesses can be a barrier to finding employment: what does a person say at an interview when they ask about the working gap in one's résumé? And how can a person find references? What if the person has a criminal record?

The system isn't arranged to support low income mentally ill people in their attempts to be independent. Continuing in this theme I will describe some obstacles I experienced myself and how subsequent failures of the system affected both, myself, and others with mental illness.

There are currently few incentives for the mentally ill who are disabled and on benefits to try to improve their economic situation. No matter your talents, intellectual or other, you might be told to be a janitor or something similar, making minimum or less wage. Now any kind of work is honorable, but not everyone has the strength to do physical labor. Everyone has their own gifts and talents and should be encouraged to use them. Working in a Goodwill store with minimal wages has its problems. For example, there is loud music played in the work place making noise pollution unbearable to cope with for many. Other times a person who has a mental illness can get a job in retail or other places that have high volume public contact, the exact opposite of what a person with mental illness needs.

As an illustration, I will describe what happened to me. I tried to work at twenty paid employment positions, both full and part-time, but failed to keep them because of not only my psychiatric disability but also because my basic needs of food and adequate clothing were not met to support me going out each day to a workplace. In addition, I lacked a supportive social network to help sustain me emotionally or psychologically, something which is fundamental to maintaining employment.

For one getting any type of job, especially part-time work while on benefits the person risks losing everything without having a safety net. Often, part-time work is the most a disabled person can do as in my own situation. One man who received Supplemental Security Income (SSI) got a paper route, which was part-time work, but he lost all his benefits leaving him eventually homeless and without medical insurance or adequate food. The paper route was not sufficient income to live on.

There are few incentives to work when you receive a small paycheck as one simultaneously have not been allowed financial gain:

1. They take away the food stamps
2. Raise your rent
3. Lower the SSI
4. You "earn" your way out of the Medicaid system, thus losing your health care coverage and with it losing necessary medications and medical/dental treatments/hospitalization coverage. The more you work over a period of time, the more you disqualify yourself from health care and the supplemental financial supports.

Of course it is a noble thing to get off food stamps and other benefits and, in the right circumstances, this is preferred. However, for the disabled who need help and who try to work, when all of the adjustments occur there is no cash in hand to show you came out ahead. All the cash earned from a paycheck does not matter because of the reduction or elimination of the above benefits which prohibits economic gain to help you climb out of poverty. Being in this system, I, personally, could not make any progress.

Early on in my efforts, I would go through the stress of getting to the work place, often using public transportation; then I had to cope with an often toxic work environment where co-workers were sometimes vicious and back-stabbing. I had to cope with symptoms of my mental illness and debilitating side-effects from medications, all the while trying to do a job that did not incorporate my talents and gifts resulting in boredom. This was all done with no reward for my efforts but, inversely, only punishment by a reduction in financial supports and no monetary gain. In other words, I didn't come out ahead—nothing to show that I had worked at all.

I tried to hold down a job without having an appropriate wardrobe, once wearing my deceased grandmother's house dress she wore to do her cleaning and cooking. I went to work hungry and battled diabetic low-blood sugar levels which caused emotional distress, while trying to cope with the additional stresses of my mental illness. The cycle of poverty continued and there was no way to make it up the ladder. To begin with, I was unable to obtain a college degree or graduate level degree before I fell ill, so I had fewer job opportunities; I could not function in a college-level educational system in order to obtain those degrees. Over the years I have pursued knowledge through self-education by extensive reading and CD/DVD college-level courses checked out from libraries.

These types of obstacles to independence are wide-spread. The mentally ill, often people without adequate food and clothing, are being told they must work in humiliating circumstances, often not able to reach a food bank because of the hours—not able, therefore, to feed themselves—and not having money for good clothes that supervisors expect them to wear in a workplace. They live below subsistence levels and are punished in their efforts to climb out of it. Abject poverty is an overused term; however, in this situation it fits. To improve the current situation, we need government laws, regulations, and newly revised programs to support those who are struggling. We need families and relatives to understand, have compassion and offer help. And most importantly, religious communities have a major part to play in providing a solid ground on which to stand, fostering a spirit of hope and healing for the ill to support a process of recovery. Without basic needs being met—physical, emotional/psychological, and spiritual—the demand for self-sufficient employment that society requires is absolutely inhumane. Most people with mental illness are not criminals. Being ill is no crime; yet the mentally ill are monitored and punished, forced to live in deprivation as though they had broken the law. The government even has access to the person's bank accounts, which are monitored, invading privacy and showing a complete lack of respect. People with mental illness are not granted even the most basic of human rights. This has got to stop!

Frequently, public attitudes toward the mentally ill hinder the rise to independence as revealed in the following illustration. In February 2012, I sent out questionnaires to the people who regularly worked on my church's designated day for the city's Free Lunch Program. The program, involving dozens of groups, serve lunch to an average of 130 people Monday through Saturday and sometimes on a Sunday for Christmas Day and New Year's. I was shocked when I read one person's comments that was in response to one of my questions which asked: "How would you describe your guests? What do you see in them? Or how do you see them?"

She replied: "I don't feel that there are really hungry people in our area. There are so many services. But we try to be pleasant to everyone, even if some are grouchy. And we encourage the regulars—many become friends."

I felt an urgent need to respond so I sent an email message to one of the coordinators of the group and asked that she share it with everyone who worked with her. I wanted to show that the difficulties regarding food scarcity for the mentally ill is a complex issue, not easily solved; and while many in our community believe we provide a wide range of "services," this is not something all lower income people can utilize, so it is not always enough.

This is what I said:

> I need to let you know that there are many people in our city who are very hungry. Some cannot access services; for example, maybe not being able to physically reach the location of the Crisis Center Food Bank which is not in a central location and they may not be able to reach the location of the mobile units for various reasons, often because of their own personal physical mobility issues, in combination with mental instability/illness, the hours the banks operate, etc. In addition, I know from the times when I've needed food from the food bank, that you need a stove top or a hot plate to cook some of the boxed and canned goods at your home. You need cooking utensils like a pot and a can opener. You may need to add extra ingredients to the mixes like milk and butter or meat which not everyone can afford. There are *many*, low income people who do not have a stove or hot plate, the additional cooking utensils or ingredients or even a home. Also, the food bank will give enough supplies for a few days for an adult, and a person can only come back once a week. I needed to have a friend drive me to the food bank and not everyone has a friend to do that. They have no transportation. The buses are not very convenient, not close to the food banks, and a person must wait outside on a street corner in all kinds of weather, sometimes for over 30 minutes to catch a bus while holding large heavy bags. To make matters worse, many do not have the bus fare. There is an aggressive group of clients who form a line outside the Crisis Center's door more than an hour before the center opens. They are the first to access the food and by the time they are done, there is little of value left over for the patrons who come later or just when the center opens.
>
> Physically getting to the Salvation Army meals (also not centrally located downtown) which are provided in the late afternoon or early evening, can be extremely difficult or even impossible for many low income people. In addition, meager food stamps allotments do not provide

enough food for a whole month, in my own case when I used them in the past, only about a week's worth of groceries. Most people run out long before the month ends. Some people don't know *how* to obtain services or where to go to access them. Some are in the process of learning, so they need a free meal in the meantime. Some are *never* able to obtain services for reasons related to physical or mental health or social conditions.

I worked as a volunteer at the very first free lunch in this program back in 1983. I set the tables and placed food on them. The counselors that started the program knew first-hand that many of their clients from the Community Mental Health Center were starving or were nearly starving. Please be assured that these conditions still exist for many in the area. The churches are providing a good hot meal for many who would perish without it. I want to thank you for your generous service and provision for all the people who suffer from the deprivations that accompany mental and physical illnesses, poverty and other life challenges. And, thanks, too, for helping the University students who come to the free lunch and others who have felt a great need for your lunches whether temporarily or on a continuous basis. Please know that what you are providing has been invaluable for thousands of people. May God grant you the strength to carry on.[17]

What I'm about to say may seem obvious, but how many of us really appreciate the problems that come with hunger? Not having enough food daily stops the forward progression of one's life. A person can be too hungry to work so they can't go to a job or maintain a usual routine. When family members will not help a disabled relative who is without resources this is the grossest inhumanity to a person. My relatives have helped me on and off, but during much of my adult years I nearly starved. There are good people running our city's food pantry and without this resource I would not have survived. And some Christians from my church have tried to make sure I've had enough food and I am grateful.

17. Author's email message to anonymous recipient, February 7, 2012.

My situation is not unique. There are many people who have a mental illness who do not have enough family support. For whatever reason, many times relatives are not aware of the problem or they deliberately turn their backs. Some place a higher value on pets—dogs, cats— over the value of a human life because they would rather poor their extra money into taking care of animals. My own siblings have had multiple cats and dogs which amount to high veterinarian fees along with maintenance, food, and boarding (when traveling) costs.

Thus, it is the religious and civic organizations which provide a safety net for the mentally ill poor, and I can testify that without them, I'd be dead. Over the course of my life I've tried to work at countless jobs and was never able to support myself. Though periodically employed and on Disability benefits, I've never made enough money for food, clothing, or shelter. The system isn't arranged to support the mentally ill low income people in their attempts to be independent. The rules, regulations, and legal restrictions are not geared to support the mentally ill in their attempts to climb out of the endless cycle of rehabilitation, recovery, work, possible relapse, hospitalization or incarceration, and finding adequate food, shelter, clothing. . . .

Why has society in general, over the centuries, turned its back on those who suffer such afflictions, leaving the mentally to languish in poverty, and ostracized, often left out and unprotected on the streets or put behind bars? What will it take to awaken people from their slumber, to awaken them to the voices of their brothers and sisters whose cries have gone unheard over a millennia, cries for justice, mercy, and a helping hand?

Chapter 2

Challenges and Reforms

Learn to do right; seek justice. Defend the oppressed.

Isaiah 1:17a (NIV)

*Speak up for those who cannot speak for themselves,
for the rights of all who are destitute.
Speak up and judge fairly;
defend the rights of the poor and needy.*

Proverbs 31:8-9 (NIV)

Dumb. Uneducated. Lazy.

Such are the stereotypes of the homeless as well as for the mentally ill in general. I am here to refute these claims. I will provide examples of men who've striven to pull themselves up from the depths of illness, yet were beaten down again by relentlessly judgmental and harsh societal attitudes.

Richard, a former high school classmate who has been chronically mentally ill and homeless for nearly forty years, is a case in point.

Richard can often be seen sitting on a bench in downtown of my city, smoking a cigarette very quietly, and seemingly deep in thought. He is of small stature, thin, wears jeans, a thin jacket, and scruffy boats. His face is worn and weathered with a complexion of a yellowish-beige tint, having endured all kinds of extreme outdoor temperatures, wind, rain, snow, and sunshine. He has stained, grayish and blackened uneven rotten teeth and scraggly hair.

I approached Richard one crisp fall morning as I was walking through Iowa City's Pedestrian Mall, a place with small shops and a children's playground. On this particular day he held a 12 x 8 inch dirty, torn, brown cardboard sign that said in large black letters, *Need Money*. I reached into my billfold, took out a dollar bill and handed it to him which, he quickly put into his pocket.

This was my second encounter with Richard over a period of several weeks. Earlier I had asked him a few questions after handing him some change: "Do you attend the free lunch?" He answered that there was a shuttle that would transport him near to where the free lunch was held, but he decided to quit going there.

"Where is the shuttle bus you mentioned the other day? You said it takes people to a corner where you can walk to the free lunch. Where do you catch that?"

Richard, at first appearing to be in a deep and peaceful calm, was quite eager to converse and friendly. He gently pointed toward the direction where the city bus interchange was located a block away and said, "It comes every fifteen minutes after the hour and goes east to Bowery and Dodge. Then you walk to the free lunch from there. Don't take the forty-five; that goes north."

"You mentioned the other day that you don't eat there now," I said.

"That's right, I used to, but decided to quit going."

"But do you have enough food to eat?"

Nodding up and down he said, "Yes, more than enough."

"Do you have an apartment?" I asked. "When it's cold—where do you stay?"

Richard paused and his eyes looked away as to a distant, possibly painful, memory. He was silent, then spoke in a hushed voice, "I have places."

"Do you have an apartment?" I asked.

"No."

"We (the city) had a winter shelter last year; did you stay there?"

He nodded.

"You stayed there?"

"Yes," he gently replied.

I continued: "Do you go to a grocery store?"

"No, people hand me a sandwich or others things as they walk by. I have more than I can eat."

I suddenly realized that I may be intruding so I said to him, "You should tell me: *'Mind your own business, woman! Mind your own business!'*"

He threw back his head and laughed.

"No, you're not bothering me; I don't mind!" And he smiled.

"I'm writing a book," I said. "I'm in recovery. I've had schizophrenia."

He quickly said, "I have schizophrenia."

"I am working to improve conditions for the mentally ill—to make things better for them in the community. What would you like to say to the community?"

Richard looked thoughtful. Then he said softly, "Thank you very much."

"Oh, I said, "You're grateful!"

"Yes." Smiling again.

Struck by how extremely pleasant and cordial Richard had been the whole time we chatted, I said, "Maybe we'll talk again some other day. I don't want to wear you out!"

"You're not wearing me out! I don't mind!"

"Maybe we can talk another day," I said.

I glanced away and rushed off down the sidewalk.

A few weeks later I traveled downtown after a Sunday church service to visit the University of Iowa Main Library. My visits and work at libraries helped me to ground myself. My work, I believed, was the purpose for my life. After I spent some time at the library, I walked up the hill to the city's deserted transit interchange, but no buses were in sight, I knew, because they don't run on Sundays. And then I spotted Richard across the street on a bench, sitting alone very quietly smoking a cigarette. It was a chilly day. He seemed to have supplies surrounding him on the bench, some type of bed-roll or wound up sleeping bag, and a few other indistinguishable items I assumed had been donated to him. The thought occurred to me: *How can he manage with carrying all those items around with him?* My immediate reaction was to go to him. I crossed the street.

I noticed the nicotine stains on his fingers as he put the cigarette to his mouth, smoke flowing gracefully around his face.

"Hi, do you remember me?"

His expression did not portray recognition, so I said, "I'm the person who talked to you a while back over on the Ped Mall. I said I was writing a book, and I asked you questions."

"Oh, yes. I think I remember." And he smiled.

"My name's Marcia. What is your name?"

Just then I saw on his face a look of immense gratitude and relief. Someone had cared enough to ask him his name.

"Richard."

He waited expectantly for more conversation, and I complied. We talked briefly for a while, and then I got a small bottle of juice out of my bag.

I reached out my hand.

"Do you like this?"

He nodded.

"Yes, I do."

"Here, you can have it," I said.

He took it from my hand.

"I'm sorry I can't give you more today."

He replied, "Oh, this is fine. Thank you very much!"

"Good-bye."

And I walked away.

To many people, the sight of Richard holding his sign quickly blurs into overall cityscape of downtown Iowa City. As passers-by avert their gaze so as not to look him in the eye, Richard becomes a nameless, story-less part of their commute to work or their lunchtime stroll. But just as nearly every pinprick light in the nighttime sky comes from a giant, ancient, flaming ball of gas trillions of miles away, every homeless person on the street, like Richard, has a name and a story of how he or she slipped through the cracks of society. As Dorieanna Dewey, former homeless outreach worker from the community mental health center, remarked:

> I believe that there is a lack of financial resources and housing to accommodate the homeless population. On the good side, I've seen a continuum of care/follow-up between many agencies in the Iowa City area. However, I still believe that many people are falling through the cracks for various reasons.[1]

I described Richard to an acquaintance of mine who said he had known Richard in high school, the same school I had attended. He said that Richard was a brilliant man. As a high school student he had achieved the highest score possible on the ACT, an exam take before admittance to a college or university. Fewer than one percent of students can obtain this level. But Richard didn't want to go to college. My source of information further told me that after high school Richard's older brother surprised him by marrying Richard's girlfriend. It was thought this had been a tremendous blow for Richard and undoubtedly a great feeling of betrayal. He moved away out of state and then returned a few months later completely psychotic.

Being emotionally devastated and mentally disabled, he was unable to obtain employment or survive on his own. Richard's brother and his wife let Richard stay with them in their home for a while, which may have further exacerbated his illness. He then left and sank into a depth of despair with total withdrawal from mainstream society. He was mentally ill with schizophrenia and unable to climb back up again from a disordered state of mind. Richard has been chronically disabled for over forty years and mostly living on the streets. He spent some time at the county home and may also have had a substance abuse problem, possibly with alcohol, as many of the homeless do. And although I appreciate Richard's thankfulness for the generosity of a few individuals each day, I can't help thinking that he further has

1. Dewey, Personal communication, April, 2012.

been betrayed by a society that has proven itself so historically ineffective of closing its many cracks.

* * *

A paradigm for understanding historical developments can be found in a model of care described in the book, *The Iowa State Psychopathic Hospital*, where an account is given of the genesis and purpose of an experimental facility with plans for construction beginning in 1910 in Iowa City. Its author, Paul E. Huston, was chairman of the University of Iowa Psychiatric Department from 1956 to 1971. He was known as a great teacher, who loved sharing knowledge with medical students, residents and those in other professions who had an interest in psychiatry and related issues—the plight of the mentally ill and the desperate need for understanding and new treatments.[2] Previously, in the late nineteenth and early twentieth century, humanitarian efforts to help the mentally ill mainly consisted of providing large institutions that ended up with only warehousing people in over-crowded conditions, which were custodial in nature—providing no medical treatments with few medical staff and in the surrounding communities, public apathy. The Great Depression of the 1930s, no doubt, was a major factor in the deprivation experienced by those in mental health facilities due to a lack of adequate funding to support the facilities operations.

The founders of the Iowa State Psychopathic Hospital originally envisioned creating a facility for the investigation into the nature, cause, and treatment of mental disease. The facility had a laboratory for neuropathology where faculty would train physicians, students, and others for how to treat the mentally ill, and it also included the training of personnel for the education of retarded children.

In 1910, few psychiatry departments existed in the medical schools across the country. It was a period of great discoveries in the physical realm of scientific medicine as well as a hopeful

---

2. Clancy, "In Memorandum," 5.

milieu across academic fields to take up the challenge of trying to discover the source of mental illness and ways to treat it. By the early 1920s, the Iowa State Psychopathic Hospital admitted people from all over the state of Iowa. Some were transferred to state institutions; however, by the 1950s, this segment to other institutions fell dramatically.³

All across the country states realized that new federal programs would support patients financially when out of institutions. So to find monetary relief, states rapidly released patients into the community. This had a detrimental effect on the patients who could not find social, financial, or community supports. This mass influx into community settings has had tragic consequences well documented elsewhere. ⁴ The mass release ushered in a new era of chronic homelessness, lack of community support, implementation of disjointed and sporadic agencies and program supports and inadequate or non-existent psychiatric medical care.

This new era has left thousands of people, like Richard, begging on streets, while others turn unsuccessfully to religious institutions and families to help them navigate their disabilities both physical and intellectual.

* * *

One chilly gray morning, I went out back taking a bag to the dumpster which was situated in the parking lot. I saw the plastic lid was open and just tossed in the bag only to be surprised. Up popped a six-foot, balding, half-naked man.

"Owww!" said the man, rubbing his head.

"Jerold! What are you doing in there?"

He was bare from the waist up.

"I'm looking for my envelope with a $300 check," Jerold said sadly.

"I hope I didn't hurt you. Are you okay?"

---

3. Huston, The Iowa State Psychopathic Hospital, 1–31 unnumbered pages

4. Torrey, *American Psychosis.*

"Yeah, I'm okay," Jerold said.

"I hope you find it," I said and walked away.

Jerold, about sixty years of age, is someone who has struggled his whole life. He has a mental illness and also is mildly intellectually impaired; his manner of speech is slightly child-like. He was unable to graduate from high school with his classmates but got his High School Equivalency Diploma in his early twenties, which he said made his mother happy. He has also struggled with occasional violent outbursts and alcohol abuse. He lives next door to my apartment building, and I have often run into him and have chatted with him outdoors.

One day I was reading in my living room when I heard loud pounding on a door that seemed to be coming from the downstairs hallway. It sounded like a man was trying to break into my neighbor's apartment. I heard the neighbor fighting back.

A deep male voice bellowed, "This is where I live! Let me in here! I live here!"

The ruckus continued, and I reached for my cell phone and dialed 911. The police soon arrived. It was Jerold! He was drunk and got confused about the location, thinking someone had locked him out of his own home. The neighbor didn't press charges, and the police got Jerold safely back inside his own apartment.

Jerold tells me that he doesn't sleep much at night. He goes out about 6 a.m. when a convenience store opens to have coffee with the proprietor whom Jerold says is his "buddy."

"Hhhiiiii, kitty-kitty. Hhhiii, kitty-kitty."

I hear Jerold calling out to the cat in his neighbor's window as he walks past.

Sometimes, Jerold and I see each other while riding the bus. He always wears sweatpants held up by red suspenders, sneakers, and carries a dark gray The North Face backpack over his shoulder, often wearing a hat. In warm seasons he might carry fishing gear and a bucket onto the bus; there is a river nearby. On this particular day, after he sat down across the aisle, he opened his mouth wide, revealing an open and rather bloody gap where his two front teeth should have been.

"Jerold! What happened?" I exclaimed.

"I was eating a Twizzler, and I broke my teeth out!"

"Maybe the Free Dental Clinic can help you," I said.

"No, I have a regular dentist I go to. I have an appointment today at eleven. When I was in the first grade, I knocked them out when I was hanging in the middle of two desks. They slid apart, and I kissed the floor!"

"Oh, my goodness," I said, "that must have hurt!"

Another time, Jerold came up to me downtown by the bus interchange and we conversed for a while sitting on a bench.

"Do you have enough food?" I asked.

"Systems Unlimited has a payee that gives me money. I go to The Catholic Worker House every Sunday for lunch."

Systems Unlimited, is an organization started in the 1970s by concerned parents of the developmentally, intellectually, and mentally disabled population. It provides many services in such areas as community and home support and sheltered work environments.[5] In Jerold's situation, there is a payee who manages his financial resources.

"How do you get to The Catholic Worker House on Sundays?" I asked, knowing it was over a mile from his home.

"I walk sometimes, but also ride my bike. I usually go to the Free Lunch all the other days but there is a man who always harasses me. He comes in drunk and attacks people. I've got my new knife here somewhere...."

Jerold reaches into his backpack, his hand searching.

"Oh! No violence, Jerold! No violence!" I said.

"If someone attacks me, I have to fight back!"

Just then a man in a bright red outfit walks up. He said something softly and indistinguishable to Jerold who just shook his head, saying, "No." The man turned and walked away.

"Who was that man, Jerold? What did he want?" I said.

"Oh, he wanted to know if I wanted any drugs."

"Oh, dear. You don't use cocaine, do you? Or meth?" I asked.

---

5. Systems Unlimited, "About Us," lines 1–4.

"No. Just sometimes some marijuana. I get so depressed because I can't find a girlfriend, and when I smoke a little marijuana, for about a half hour I forget about it and feel really good. But I don't do that much. I have to go now; I'm catching the bus. I walk my brother's two dogs every day. It's my job; he pays me. He lives over by the mall. Then I walk over to the free lunch to eat."

In addition to the fellowship and spiritual nourishment he experiences at the Catholic Worker House during Sunday meals, Jerold has tried to join several other religious communities. I saw him, one Sunday morning, being given a ride from a local church, as a car waited for him in the parking lot. Jerold came out in a good-looking suit and tie. Later on, I asked him about it.

"Jerold, did you like the church you attended for a worship service? Were the people nice and friendly to you? I see this church provides transportation," I said.

"Oh, I quit going. Yeah, they were nice. It was hard to meet people. You just call the church, and they give you a ride."

"Did anyone talk to you there?"

"Yeah, some did. I just don't want to go now."

"Maybe you can try it again sometime. That is really nice that they give you a ride."

I admire Jerold for being this brave. As a person with his disabilities, both intellectual and psychiatric, he might have felt quite a bit different than the congregation of this church. And going with a person he doesn't know beforehand in their car and sitting alone in the sanctuary would have taken a lot of courage. I'm sad he doesn't feel able to continue. I hope he can connect through other avenues with the body of Christ.

* * *

An improvement on the Johnson County Poor Farm was the construction of Chatham Oaks, a facility built next door in 1964. Though originally run by the county, in 2011 it was privately owned and operated which was when I toured the place. My guide was an employed social worker who seemed full of energy and vitality. By contrast, many of the residents of the facility looked rather withdrawn and aimless. The facility appeared very clean and orderly, showing it was well taken care of. The dining area was attractive and pleasant with a screened in porch with tables and chairs. There was a menu posted on a sign out front so the residents could see their dietary choices. A woman was seated directly outside smoking on the patio. After viewing the dining area, we went down to the basement where there were more residents, some sitting quietly and chatting while others were doing exercises led by a physical therapist. This was similar to what you might see at an elderly center where the people sit on chairs and just move their arms.

The basement was spacious for watching TV or playing games, there was a chess board and exercise machines. To the back was a dimly lit, small library room. It had in it several shelves of books and some bare tables where a woman sat quietly reading. There was also a computer room. I was told that a counselor would periodically hold classes in the basement on subjects such as "self-esteem" or "anger management."

There was a little canteen and something called a bank room which was where they could withdraw some cash from their allowance. The social worker said the residents were allowed a small amount of spending money each month. They could buy candy, ice cream, and pop between meals. There was a hair styling salon where they could get haircuts for eleven or twelve dollars.

The laundry area was also in the basement along with a storage room. A former employee told me a story that on one occasion a snake was seen hanging from a pipe in the laundry room; another time a snake was seen crawling up the stairway from the basement. This is quite conceivable because Chatham Oaks is on the outskirts of town at the country's edge where a lot of critters live who could make their way through the ground and foundation of this building.

We took an elevator to an upper floor that held the bedroom areas divided by genders, with six beds to a room. In one of the rooms some clients were sleeping even though it was a little past 10 a.m. Our guide said the management doesn't want to force the residents to get up if they are tired, but they do encourage them to get out of the rooms during the day. Down the hall from the bedrooms was a day room with windows and a TV and chairs. It appeared to be a quiet place for the residents.

I asked the social worker how many people stay there permanently and how many people transition through, moving out into the community. At the time of this tour, some residents would stay for a few weeks to a month, others would stay about six months, and the rest would be there for long term.

It looked to me like the residents of Chatham Oaks were well taken care of. Every month a psychiatrist would see patients there along with nursing staff and other social workers. In one wing was a nurse's medication room where residents came daily for what they were prescribed. Before residents were released to live in the community they were checked in the kitchen area to see if they could cook their own meals.

The care offered by Chatham Oaks was a big step up from the Poor Farm insane asylum where clients were just locked up in a bare cell with little provisions: inadequate food and water, no warm clothes or adequate protection from freezing temperatures in the winter and exposure to heat in summer. Chatham Oaks has central air conditioning and, of course, winter heating. The residents have ample food, clothing, and the company of other people. They have therapists who are working to help them to either recover or to stabilize. This facility which has provided care for those with psychiatric illness as well as those with intellectual disabilities is a big leap forward from what existed in the mid-nineteenth and early twentieth centuries.

But Chatham Oaks has a limited number beds and they keep decreasing due to cuts in county funding. The service offered by this exemplar facility cannot keep up with the growing needs within Johnson County, let alone within the state of Iowa. At best it offers a respite for people transitioning from living on the street to finding a place to live and a sense of purpose that gives them more stability.

Challenges and Reforms

* * *

It was a warm summer morning, and I had just stepped out of the public library when I came upon Len, an acquaintance of twenty-some years. Len is a single man, six feet tall and bespectacled, about sixty years in age. Usually clean shaven, today he had a couple of days' worth of uneven growth with remnants of food on his chin. Across his wrinkled shirt, drippings from breakfast created a mad, disorderly appearance. We greeted one another, then I just couldn't help myself, and feeling very compelled I blurted out:

"Do you have a job?!"

The reason I asked was because he seemed so aimless and lost—not just today but for some of the preceding weeks that I had noticed him. Len appeared to have no purpose in life and was just wandering about ceaselessly downtown day after day. I had experienced the value of work in my volunteering over the years. Work had given me structure for my day and helped me to feel useful part of the time. A job also helped me to feel I was contributing to something greater than myself—getting my mind off myself with a focus on goals and tasks. Work brought much needed social interaction as well.

Len looked startled.

"You are a very intelligent woman," he said.

"I just think you'd feel better if you had a job, some work to do, even just a couple of hours."

"Yes, you're probably right. I'll think about it," he said and walked away.

A few weeks later I got on the bus heading home and Len was there and he looked different. He was well-groomed with a spotless, rather dressy shirt; his face was clean shaven. He was sitting up straight.

"Hi, Len," I said, "How are you? You look great!"

I took the seat behind him and he twisted slightly to the side to chat.

"I am volunteering now. Once a month I work with St. Mary's group on Fridays serving at the Free Lunch. I also work on

Wednesdays and the other Fridays at the Crowded Closet Clothing Store, cleaning the rooms, vacuuming and sweeping the floors. I enjoy doing that."

The Crowded Closet is a relief organization of the Mennonite church. It serves low income people by selling inexpensive donated clothing and household items. I told Len that it is great he found some work he enjoys.

He said, "I don't feel able now to give an employer a good full day's work like I used to. So I am volunteering part-time."

"That's very nice," and I congratulated him.

Len is not a lazy person. He is up at the crack of dawn every day; he always has been even when unemployed. He takes the first scheduled bus in the morning downtown and buys a cup of coffee. He doesn't sit at home watching TV. He doesn't smoke or drink alcohol. He is usually very mild mannered and conversant though he confessed to me his problems with occasional violence, once, for example, when defending a homeless woman against an aggressor. He socializes with other people who have a mental illness, sharing coffee or meals in restaurants. Len has always wanted employment. He started working when he was in high school for a grocery chain in the evenings while trying to keep up with his school work during the day. He attended a Catholic high school and then a public college, majoring in engineering. He was good at math but had to drop out before getting his degree. Even though he came down with schizophrenia his attitude toward work continued to be exemplary. He had a succession of jobs mostly in grocery stores.

"When I worked at the grocery store a while back, I lost my temper once. So that was the end of that job," Len told me.

Quite often, Len will explain to me his latest ideas for trying to run a business. He thinks up gadgets or contraptions he'd like to build or a service he could provide if he would find a partner to provide some capital and investment. He tells me I'm great for bouncing ideas off of because I always ask good questions that help him to organize his thoughts.

Challenges and Reforms

We sometimes come across each other at the coffee shop. Once we took our coffee cups out to a bench on the Ped Mall and sat discussing a wide variety of topics: his early childhood education by nuns, St. Augustine and his *City of God*, and the Russian novelist Dostoyevsky and his *Brothers Karamazov*. When not pacing the streets, Len can be seen sitting on a bench or standing in front of a woman's clinic praying his rosary, and he likes to check in on a friend who is a Vet and suffers from mental illness. Len feels obligated to care for him. He also tells me of his frequent visits to the campus Catholic center where he participates in worship services. I've seen him dressed for mass wearing a long handsome black overcoat.

Another day on the bus, when we were traveling to different but near destinations, we had a minute to talk. Len told me, "Leaders need to be peacemakers." He then shared that he had given the rabbi of the local Jewish synagogue a donation of $150 and had asked the rabbi to give it to the poorest family in their congregation. Len has a very limited income, so this was a substantial sacrifice and gift. Just then the bus went by a small apartment complex, and Len said, "I lived there in an apartment for twenty-five years."

"Yes," I said. "Didn't Pam help you find it?"

Len had been homeless even though he tried to work and be fully employed when a mental health counselor went to bat for him and found him the apartment. He has since moved across town to a safer neighborhood after being threatened.

"Yes, she did," Len said. "All I want is a warm room in the winter. That's all I want."

* * *

During the first half of the nineteenth century many of the mental patients in US asylums were literally naked—not provided with clothing—as pictured in Life Magazines exposé, "Bedlam 1946," at Byberry Hospital near Philadelphia.[6] Fast forward to the twenty-first century and we still find patients are desperate for clothing both

---

6 Philadelphia State Hospital, "Opacity," lines 23–28.

during their stay while on psychiatric units as well as when living on the streets. The public's apathy has diminished only slightly. My religious organization, the Presbyterian Church, (USA), has responded to my clothing drives for psychiatric in-patients with generous hearts in recent years. I have a collaboration with a state hospital to bring the clothing items to the units. However, this example needs replication around the entire country with both religious and civic organizations stepping up to the challenge. I'd say there is a place for patience and a place for impatience. Overall, when less privileged individuals are without clothes, housing, or health care due to the neglect, apathy, and indifference of the *haves* this is worse than overt, visible, and direct violence. Neglect is an invisible, passive violence, and because of its invisible nature it is then more profoundly administered, cruel, and destructive.

The system isn't arranged to support low income people in their attempts to be independent. First of all, there needs to be a foundation of good psychiatric care without which recovery is not likely to occur. In the 1960s and 70s, the University of Iowa Psychiatric Hospital (formerly, The Iowa State Psychopathic Hospital), had established compassionate treatment for the ill and though it was soon replaced by insurance-driven short-term care, this previous model is an example of how the ingenuity and resourcefulness of medical professionals provided a healing environment. I will describe this facility now at length gleaned from my own experience there as a patient (three admissions between 1976 and 1985) and a supplemental interview with psychiatric nurse (RN, now retired), Jean McCarty.[7]

The University of Iowa Psychiatric Hospital contained two wards, the East and West, holding twenty-eight patients on each. Stays averaged about a month during which time the patients were given treatment and were evaluated to see whether they could be released out into the community or if they needed long-term care in a state mental health institution. But the primary aim was mostly to give psychiatric care and treatments, more than simply an evaluation. The majority were then sent back into the community.

---

7. McCarty, author interview, January 12, 2001.

Originally, there were both a women's and men's unit; then in the early 1970s they were mixed with a slightly higher number of women than men. Adults were admitted from age eighteen and the most predominate age group in the facility was the late twenties to forty, with a few older. A patient was first examined by a physician at the in-take room which was located in the basement before being admitted to a ward at a ground floor level. Besides the physical exam, the physician would do a mental status to see if the patient was aware of their surroundings and what was going on in the world. The physician would ask for symptoms, what brought the patient to the hospital, what medication they had been on, what they've been doing at home: has the patient's behavior changed? When a family member was present the physician asked for their perspective, especially if the patient was not thinking clearly. The patient and/or family members were asked if alcohol was involved and were there any prior illnesses or hospitalizations.

Once admitted, patients usually spent their time in the day room, a spacious and open indoor area where patients gathered during waking hours. It had several comfortable chairs with a couch in the middle. A non-functioning fireplace was on a side wall and there was a shelf with games, magazines, and picture puzzles. Long, screened windows without bars let in ample sunlight. An attractive area rug covered the main area of this room and a clean, hard surface was throughout other parts of the unit.

Upon being admitted a registered nurse questioned the patient, asking whether they felt depressed, did they hear voices, whether the patient was physically active, if they were sleeping and eating well, and did they feel suicidal or homicidal. The nurse asked about a social history and found out who to call in case of an emergency, who the patient was living with if anyone, who gave the patient support. A social worker would do an extensive and comprehensive social history which after several years has been eliminated. For a while each patient had their own social worker, then later on only if a patient had a special reason for needing one. Testing done by a psychologist was only done by special order of a physician as was participation in group therapy.

The patient was allowed to wear their own clothing unless they were on elopement precautions (which meant they might run out the door if they had the opportunity). The thought was that wearing a hospital gown would make it less appealing to be out in the community. Elopement of a patient occurred about one every month or two. They would either leave the unit somehow or from an outdoor activity. Staff, campus security or police would then hunt them down.

Soon after admission the doctor ordered tests (i.e., drew blood) to determine whether the patient had the afflictions of malnutrition, thyroid problems, electrolytes imbalance, plus an EKG was done. In addition, a chest x-ray was done if the patient was to have ETC's (electroconvulsive therapy) where seizures are electronically induced.

Since this was a teaching facility one resident and one medical student were assigned to meet with the patient every morning, and the staff doctor met a few times a week. Social workers, dieticians, and nurses also met with the patient to develop a treatment plan. By a doctor's order, a psychologist might administer tests with the patient. There were occupational and activity (recreational) therapists and also as part of the social work department, a person from Vocational Rehabilitation. A hair solon was on the unit with a stylist staffed daily.

The medical records were created by daily notes from physicians, nurses, and nursing assistants written at the end of each shift. These were kept in a large, round metal chart rack on a table in the center of the nursing station that had a unit clerk. This station was a rectangular room with windows on two sides into the ward, built-in desks, and telephones. The room also had a small refrigerator and a sink. Entrance into the station was by a large wooden door that had a top half which swung open to allow the dispensation of meds which were placed on a ledge for the patients. The pills were given out around nine o'clock at night in little soufflé cups along with a cup of water. A nurse and two nursing assistants staffed each unit over-night. A physician would be in-house, or on-call.

Challenges and Reforms

Patients were encouraged to be out of their rooms as much as possible during the day. Sometimes, however, the medication would make the patient too groggy and so they couldn't get up out of bed. There were activities in the morning and then a rest period right after lunch followed by an activity, then a late afternoon activity at four o'clock. A television set and chairs were in the vestibule of the ward, an enclave near the entrance with large pleasant windows. Soothing views of trees, blue sky, and birds in flight had a calming effect. The TV was allowed on until 11:30 p.m. weeknights, and 12:30 a.m. weekends.

Down a hall of one wing was a sun room, a screened in porch near the front of the building with a ping pong table which was also where patients could smoke cigarettes as they were provided with electric wall-mounted lighters. There was a telephone room in a small room down an opposite hallway that was always kept locked. The staff would monitor the length of calls and notify patients when a call was coming in. Bathing was allowed after seven o'clock in the morning. There was a bathtub and showers. Patients had to be supervised when using the tub. The patients were provided soap, towels, tooth-paste, and a tooth-brush. They were also provided with their own hair-brush and comb which could be kept in the patient's room in a chest drawer. When under supervision, people could shave with razors, or use an electric razor unsupervised.

In occupational therapy patients worked on crafts and in recreational therapy they were taken to a gym on-site or driven to a bowling alley or ice cream shop in the community. Outings included visiting parks that were a few miles away. One of the afternoon activities was music therapy and at times this included going out to a nearby neighborhood to watch the University's marching band practicing in a field.

Patients were awakened individually by staff each morning around seven o'clock. Breakfast was at eight. Medications were given out between eight and nine. Then the first activity was at nine. Lunch-time was at eleven-thirty followed by rest-time, then activities, and dinner was at five. Meals in the dining room were served family-style on six round tables. Snack carts were on the unit three times a day. Patients were provided with plenty of wholesome food and drinks at regular intervals which consisted of good protein sources, fresh fruit, dairy products and vegetables.

There were groups led by staff for patients to work on various things such as depression and inter-personal skills. A patient could earn privileges and passes for going out of the ward. There were various activity levels. The first level when admitted was *restricted* and then after two days they were moved up to *supervised*. If the patient wasn't suicidal they could go out with a friend or family and stay out even over a weekend. Then the level was moved up to *routine*, which is when the patient is allowed off the unit by themselves for an hour twice a day. There was an activity level called *blue card* where students who wanted to go to class all day could attend those but they had to make sure they got their medications and kept any appointments in the hospital.

At the back of the East Ward there was a room for ECT (shock treatments) which also contained table and a crash cart consisting of emergency equipment. ECT was used to treat depression and catatonic schizophrenia—when the patient was immobile and could not eat or drink or move about freely.

A quiet room on each unit was behind a locked door. Patients who were out of control, disruptive, and loud needed to be confined to keep others safe. It had plastic and a sheet and blanket covering a mattress on the floor with a pillow. A large skeleton key locked the door which hung outside. The room was not sound proof so at times angry shouting and distraught cries could be heard throughout the unit. Sometimes such confinement was necessary due to the violent nature or episodic outbursts which put others on the unit in danger. The safety of the unit had to be maintained.

Regardless of the presence of a quiet room in this period of psychiatric history, the rest of the preceding summary shows a great leap forward in humane treatment of the mentally ill. The facility was closed in 1991 when units were relocated to the main hospital into newly constructed areas. During my stay in the older hospital I experienced how patients were provided compassionate care by trained hospital personnel who most likely felt personally compelled to provide the best treatments available. The very practice of allowing a month (or longer) stays in the facility while exploring numerous treatment options reveals a patience and thoroughness in regard to a holistic healing of body, mind, and spirit. How tragic is the current state of affairs regarding the length of hospital stays often with limits of five to six days dictated by insurance. Now in current times, the former great depth of care is curtailed by insurance which places huge restrictions on what doctors can and cannot do in order help this most vulnerable and desperate of populations.

* * *

Sixty miles east of Johnson County, a Davenport, Iowa, newspaper, *The Daily Gazette*, published an article on April 20, 1873, about the disastrous conditions of their poor house in which not only paupers, but also those disabled and afflicted in both body and mind were being confined.[8] Newspaper correspondents from around the region decried the immoral and cruel conditions under which powerless people were forced to live, in not only dilapidated buildings and unsanitary living quarters, but in abusive situations "beyond description."[9]

Stating when directing funds to improve conditions that *money will not buy sympathy,*" the county officials received an offer from *Sisters of Mercy*, a Catholic organization of women from the city of nearby DeWitt, a group bonded together with a focus of helping those on the fringes of society, the helpless and most in need of assistance.[10] The Sisters had become aware of the desperate condition of the mentally ill in the Scott County poor house and with great compassion told the authorities they were willing to care for these people by setting up an insane asylum in the vicinity of Davenport. Thus Mercy Hospital became the place where the

8. Watkins, "A Necessary Institution," 4.
9. Ibid.
10. Ibid.

Sisters took care of the homeless insane and without any monetary reward. A request was being made through this article for public financial support to pay a debt that had accrued for the care of the insane in this asylum.[11]

Over a decade later, the Linn County supervisors in the city of Cedar Rapids, thirty miles north of Iowa City, express the wish to keep the insane closer to within city limits rather than the state institution several more miles away which is more costly.[12] An *Evening Gazette* article of July 28, 1887, discusses the business aspect of providing for the insane and reveals the priority of decision-making based on the best economy.[13] It appears that much of the thinking is based on financial considerations and how to best serve the mentally ill population at the lowest cost.[14]

The mentally ill at this time, unable to care for themselves, represented a burden to the rest of society and much time and effort was spent on how society could relieve themselves, as much as possible, of this burden. In the 1800s, little effort was made to aid those in distress other than the most basic custodial support. It is apparent that that the economic problem was a stronger priority than making the moral choice of providing compassionate, loving, care to heal mental and spiritual devastation inherit in all aspects of psychiatric disorder.

What does it take to put a human face on mental illness? When will society see the mentally ill as human beings, made in the image of God like you and me, those born of a mother, the childhood friend, the co-worker, and someone next to us on a pew who yearns for acceptance, validation as a child of God?

11. Ibid.
12. Davis and Bunting, "The Poor Farm Matter," 2.
13. Ibid.
14. Ibid.

Chapter 3

Civility, Grace, and Mental Health

Bullying   *Using force or violence against; abuse and mistreatment of someone vulnerable*

Civility   *Politeness, courtesy in behavior/speech. Treating others with respect, consideration*

Grace   *Unmerited favor; unconditional love*

THE NINETEENTH CENTURY REFORMERS, I am sure, congratulated themselves upon completing construction of the insane asylum wing. After all, they were providing a place to house the mentally ill, though inadequately from my viewpoint. These good intentions were insufficient. The mentally ill, in a very real sense, were treated as less than human: ostracized from the community, as the asylum had been built on the outskirts of the city. They were cut off from social interactions that could have helped to build them up. Instead they were left to deteriorate mentally and spiritually—prevented from church attendance, unable to receive the sacrament of communion, as well as fellowship within the body of Christ. Inmates—I will call them "inmates," for that was, indeed, all they amounted to be—experienced emotional distress and humiliation: lack of intellectual stimulation or mental exercise, lack of privacy. Being locked in cells like criminals they were also prevented from physical exercise and proper hygiene. All of these things led to a further deterioration of mental conditions and, I'm sure, utter hopelessness. Although the reformers had not consciously intended abuse, their inadequate provisions amounted to nothing more than that—leading to greater depths of insanity for the inmates. These deprivations exacerbated the initial symptoms of mental illness, preventing any kind of recovery.

In the book, *Our Most Troubling Madness: case studies in schizophrenia across cultures*, contributing editors T.M. Luhrmann and Jocelyn Marrow maintain that both physical and mental deprivations along with bullying, criticism (being judged negatively), and devalued or looked down on, induces mental distress which can, and often does, lead to mental illness.[1] I agree with this premise and though there are exceptions, abuse can be a substantial factor in the etiology of psychiatric illness. *Our Most Troubling Madness* describes several anthropologists' field research exploring what recovery looks like across cultures. The anthropologists doing the field research for these studies were not psychiatrists, they were investigating as non-medical personnel. Even so, they felt justified to make their own opinions regarding practices and treatments for the mentally ill. They stated that environments shape beliefs about what psychosis is or is not; and how groups, i.e., familial, religious, and societal, play a part in the genesis of illness, as well as how communities respond to a mentally ill person, often resulting in certain detrimental outcomes. Is a person with a psychosis loved or bullied? Supported or rejected? Protected or abandoned? The milieu of the home environment, work place and other public spaces, can, and often does, influence the mental health of individuals who must interact in such places.[2]

Psychological abuse (also referred to as psychological violence), is a form of mistreatment characterized by a person subjecting or exposing another person to behavior that may result in psychological trauma including anxiety, chronic depression, psychosis, or post-traumatic stress disorder.[3]

1. Luhrmann, Marrow, eds., *Our Most Troubling Madness*, 201–3.
2. Ibid.
3. Psychological abuse, Wikipedia, lines 1–3.

CIVILITY, GRACE, AND MENTAL HEALTH

I would add that in conjunction, these social-environmental factors set the stage for any pre- and co- existing physiological/neurological stresses in the brain that can, and often do, malfunction, leading to a major mental breakdown. Breakdowns can occur at any time: in childhood, teen years and later on into the adult years. What kind of social-environmental conditions existed for people in mid-American during the nineteenth century? The Johnson County poor farm and insane asylum is a good expression of this time period for this society's response to people that struggled with mental illness.

It appears that nineteenth century reformers who built the county home and insane asylum wing lacked empathy for how the inmates suffered within such a bare, Spartan facility. Whatever good intentions, the stringent living conditions for the inmates would attest that the reformers cared little for how the inmates experienced their confinement. Otherwise, there would have been a greater attention to providing modest comforts. The extreme weather conditions, alone, created great obstacles for those confined within the thin walls of the asylum.

> *Empathy is something we have that allows us to understand how other people feel. This is something that allows us to become more sensitive to the needs and feelings of others. We will then be more likely to help those who are hurt or troubled—treating others with compassion . . . It stops us from acting in a cruel manner.*[4]

I know had I been confined in this asylum, that such conditions would have driven me further insane than how I had started out at the beginning of being placed there. And recovery? Completely out of the question. It is likely that some of the inmates of the asylum had behavior issues including violence, and were uncontrollable while living in the community. And confinement was the last resort. The way the inmates behaved must have been a big factor in their options of shelter; however, the way they were treated by the city leaders also had a strong bearing upon potential

---

4. Borba, *Building Moral Intelligence*, 6.

outcomes. These living conditions would only destroy what little health the inmates had, leading only to death itself and most likely a welcome death, too.

* * *

Human interaction, verbal and behavioral, is an often neglected factor in the epidemiology of psychiatric disorders in our age of pharmaceutical interventions. I propose that there is a strong connection between social environments and mental health outcomes. My own parents struggled financially and were constantly working, which left them with little free time to be with my siblings and me. I know they tried to provide for us the best they could and I'm grateful for everything I had while growing up. But as it turns out, my own experience of a dysfunctional home life made it less likely that I could learn the proper way to behave and make choices which come after considering options. As I grew into adulthood I needed to develop insight and learn to monitor my own behavior patterns, to unlearn bad ways of thinking and behaving, and to consciously learn and adopt healthy ones instead.

As is well known, often in dysfunctional families a cycle of abuse can continue through future generations. In order to halt this cycle it is helpful for individuals who have been mistreated to recognize not only when this has happened, but to consciously make positive changes within themselves, to unlearn destructive behavior patterns and build new and healthier ones. As I grew into adulthood I learned that ethical development and learning moral behaviors were to become key elements in my own recovery from mental illness and in how I interacted with the world. For example: knowing right from wrong, making good choices, acting in accordance with ethical decisions; obtaining a strong internal locus of control with the ability to carry out decisions; maintaining integrity so others can count on me to do what I say I will do and in consistency in moral choices—not vacillating on a day to day basis. These were all new behaviors I needed to learn and practice.

Discarding negative thinking and choices, I gradually adopted these elements of good mental health: doing no harm to others

Civility, Grace, and Mental Health

and respecting the rights of others; treating others with patience and kindness; meeting everyday situations with a sense of justice and fairness; having compassion for those less fortunate, i.e., the suffering, weak, excluded, and those who are less privileged. In addition I found that maintaining good ethics and morality leading to good emotional health would involve refraining from sexual immorality and/or promiscuity as well as refraining from smoking, abuse of alcohol and other substances.

One morning I saw on the local news a segment about a man who allegedly attacked a woman who was walking down the street. He forced her into a house where he brutally beat, sexually assaulted, and killed her. When the police finally caught up with him and he was questioned, he confessed to the crime and reportedly said: "I had nothing better to do."[5] This man lacked a conscience. What is conscience?

> *Conscience is knowing the right and decent way to act and carrying it out. The inner voice that helps us know right from wrong—which is at the foundation for ethical behavior, decent living, and solid citizenship. It's what morality is all about; together with empathy and self-control, it's one of the three cornerstones of moral intelligence.*[6]

The man who allegedly attacked this woman was obviously not kind. In stark contrast he was cruel and uncaring. In our society today how often do we see kindness displayed in our relations with others not only within our families but out in the broader society, our work places, and public spaces in general? How do we describe kindness?

> *Kindness is acting in such a way that shows concern about the welfare and feelings of others. Acts of kindness are what build civility, humaneness, and morality. What kind people do: Stick up for someone being teased; offer to help someone in need; show concern when someone is sad; refuse to be part of ridiculing others; pay attention to others' concerns; think about the needs of others; behave*

---

5. Hanson, "Trial Must Be Moved," KWWL, lines 1–11.
6. Borba, *Building Moral Intelligence*, 51–53.

in a manner that makes others happy; show concern when someone is treated in an unkind way.[7]

One example of kindness is when I became ill with fibromyalgia. Fibromyalgia is a chronic neurologic medical condition that causes pain all over the body. In addition, other symptoms are: tenderness to touch or pressure affecting muscles and sometimes joints or even the skin; severe fatigue; sleep problems (waking up unrefreshed); problems with memory or thinking clearly; depression and/or anxiety; migraine or tension headaches.[8]

I do not own a vehicle and a friend I had met at church took it upon herself to assist me. Originally, a few years earlier when I severely injured my shoulder and arm, this friend volunteered to drive me to the grocery store and then carried heavy sacks up stairs and into my apartment. As my body continued to break down in the pain and weakness associated with fibromyalgia she continued to help. Though a busy wife, mother, and career woman (a professional at the University), she still carved out time to help me get food and supplies. When I have been even more ill or immobilized, she has brought over home-made soups. Her generosity has been remarkable. We also celebrate birthdays and other special occasions together. She has been Christ to me.

Another example of kindness is in my next door neighbor, Ross, a quiet, reserved, thoughtful faculty member at the University. One day I noticed him standing at the bus stop, a NAMI tote bag in his hand. NAMI stands for National Alliance on Mental Illness, a grass roots organization working to support and advocate for and with people who have a mental illness.[9] Over the next several months I got to know Ross by chatting while waiting for the bus. He shared with me his struggles with depression. Even though most of his adult life he had been able to support himself, there was a short period when he had almost starved. Soon after Ross moved into the area he got involved in a neighborhood

---

7. Ibid., 158, 163.
8. American College of Rheumatology, "What is Fibromyalgia?" lines 1–11.
9. NAMI, "About NAMI," lines 1–3.

church and became a more cheerful personality. He has expressed his enjoyment of this religious organization; I think his religious faith is a great help for him.

During a cold winter morning I found that my budget could not afford adequate food for my needs that month so I decided to try going to a nearby mobile food pantry which came on a certain day. I realized my legs could not even make it that far because of the fibromyalgia and my shoulder was still not healed from its earlier injury. I asked Ross if he could possibly drive me there and back. He graciously agreed and did so. To reciprocate, I gave Ross a bit of gas money and every once in a while cooked a casserole for him.

Other kind people from my religious organization have also stepped up to bat in my times of need. When I have been ill, friends have gone to the pharmacy to pick up my medications or have driven me there so I could get them. And several church members, including some from another Presbyterian church across town, have driven me places for meetings, events, and doctor appointments. Many good people have given me rides for church services on Sunday mornings.

The opposite of kindness is cruelty. Cruelty can be curbed by role models, such as, parents, teachers, pastors, rabbis, and others who will teach children how to love others and how to be kind. Such authority figures can exemplify what it's like to be a caring human being, showing examples of positive ethical and moral behavior which is a hallmark of good mental health. When children and adults are recipients of kindness they themselves are more apt to display kindness in the way they interact with others.

Building bigger and better jails is a topical band aid for many of our social problems when what we need is open-heart surgery. Let's get to the heart of the matter for how to solve gun violence and other serious social ills. What is inside a person is learned as a child in the home, religious organizations, and schools. Intrinsic motivation for living is what counts and when this is guided by a good moral compass exemplified in a kind and generous heart toward others, then societal problems are lessened. Then human life is valued. Sanctity of life becomes the norm, not strife, envy and power-plays. It starts in the home and religious organizations, branching out into schools and as an adult, into the work place.

When families, religious organizations, and schools have these positive characteristics there is much less likelihood that a child growing up in these social environments will become mentally disturbed or ill. Please be aware that there are exceptions to this premise. As one example, a family unit can be healthy but one or more family member might develop a hubristic self-image which can be described as a condition of exaggerated importance, pride, and egocentricism, building up quite often into a psychosis. For the purposes of this current discussion I will focus not on hubris, but on mental illness as caused by factors of a social environment consisting of critical, humiliating, and bullying behavior directed toward a vulnerable and powerless family member, which includes but is not limited to, neglect and deprivation (lack of positive stimulus and emotional support as well as physical malnourishment). A weaker family member who is so injured mentally, emotionally, and sometimes, physically, can develop a mental illness and receive injuries resulting in permanent lifelong psychological damage.

Beyond the family and as an outgrowth of a healthy family system, how can we within the church engage in healthy social interactions? The Bible contains lessons that members of religious and educational organizations can exemplify in their behaviors and can teach to others. I will not sanitize the Church. I was brought up in a Lutheran church as a child; when I went back to a protestant church as an adult I found it difficult to connect socially with members. It took me many years, but after I self-published my first book, *Voices in the Rain: Meaning in Psychosis*, about my life, struggles with psychosis, and my recovery process, some people in the church I attended read the book and several became friendly. They seemed a little more understanding and I felt some acceptance. I was invited to give presentations in the church and we invited other speakers who advocated for the disabled as well.

Civility, Grace, and Mental Health

Over the years I have been hoping that the milieu will begin to change to something beyond mere tolerance to a place of belonging. However in order to reach such a place of belonging I still face some challenges along the way. There are occasions when discrimination has resulted in verbal conflicts and a lack of understanding has resulted in hurt feelings. There are still times when I feel devalued and when I am not treated respectfully. Overall, my church experience has been a constant struggle, and has been more of an exercise of the heart, forgiving and being forgiven—it works both ways—each extending the love of God and grace to others.

To illustrate some difficulties I will share the following. This is something that has been problematic: Church staff and sometimes committee members have neglected to respond to my concerns regarding my church ministries, the work I am doing; or in some cases they have delayed communications regarding my email inquiries without any initial acknowledgements at all. Sometimes, responses have been evasive and do not address my concerns.

Whatever the reason, this pattern with problems of communication is something which the church needs to address. How do we respond to one another in a respectful, prompt, and courteous way? When I have sent straight forward inquiries the proper response would be to initially acknowledge them; and if there will be an evaluation process on their end regarding my concern, and that process would need to take place over a period of time, it would be important for this to be explained and that I would be notified eventually when a decision has been made. Neglecting to provide any kind of response at all is insensitive and disrespectful. Then people are left hanging—are left in the dark and feeling unacknowledged, or worse yet, discriminated against. Men, especially, need to be civil and treat women respectfully.

Another example is more significant. Upon reflection, I believe I have been able to forgive, and I have since the incident, tried to understand what transpired. The relationship issues have since been somewhat resolved but situations still pop up. It is taking time to learn how to work together but unfortunately, this has be going on for over twenty years with little improvement. I will share the following to illustrate another of these challenges.

When I first founded my Mental Health Initiatives program at the church I attend, I have to admit that it got off to a rather bumpy start. One summer, I approached a certain committee requesting to show a PowerPoint slideshow for the church Adult Ed class. It was on the topic of the plight of the mentally ill and what the church can do. It was a lot of hard work and took over six months to create. I had invested a great amount of emotional energy into the project. I described some of my own struggles with mental illness and how the church has a key role in supporting the mentally ill population in various ways. Survival issues for someone with mental illness is not well publicized so I was hoping to educate and inform my church community about how this needs to be addressed.

A committee member responded by saying that they would arrange a preview of the slideshow with a couple of representatives from the committee; then this group would decide if the slideshow could be presented in Adult Ed for a Sunday in January which was the church's designated Mission Month. It was now early August and I waited for them to contact me. I waited through the entire month of August for notification of the meeting to view the slideshow. Nothing. September—nothing. October—nothing. November—nothing. December arrived and I was more than a bit anxious. I sent emails. A committee member responded to me in late December and said that during a specified two week period, we would use an on-line sign-up program and the participating committee members, along with one of the pastors, would indicate what day they are free to preview the slideshow. If no one could agree to meet on a specific day during this two week period, the committee member said the whole project would be totally dropped. I was devastated.

As the first week progressed with no one yet signing up (except me), my anxiety presented itself in the physical form of headaches and nausea. With great trepidation I learned that one of the two committee members who was assigned to attend the meeting

Civility, Grace, and Mental Health

didn't know how to use the computer sign-up program. At the end of this first week I phoned the church secretary and explained with a tremendous sense of urgency the situation about the project facing rejection if the preview meeting was not organized within seven days. She said she would do something. A few days later I talked to her again and she said she had gotten on the phone with all of the people involved and was able to set up a day and time for the preview to take place. She accomplished this within seventy-two hours of the deadline.

The committee members had had an entire five months prior to January to arrange the viewing. Instead, they had planned to cancel my project if the arrangement could not be made within a narrow two week time span at the end of December by people who either didn't know how to use the on-line sign-up program or who refused to use it. Without the last minute intervention of the church secretary, my project and the foundation for my mental health ministry might never have gotten off the ground at all within the Church as a whole.

So forgiveness was in order. I must admit that, for me, forgiveness can sometimes be a rather slow and gradual process. As it turns out, they did preview the slideshow that late December day and it was approved. I held my Adult Ed class in January and was soon invited to present the same thing again for a senior group at church and a few months later also for a Methodist women's group in a near-by town. I then posted the slide-show at my website and my personal YouTube channel and it is also now available on my church's website. The Mental Health Initiatives ministry went forward and became what it is today.

I've mentioned the church, but this topic also refers to the work situation involving supervisors, colleagues and co-workers. Is it all competition at work and power plays? Or is there a spirit of cooperation and mutual respect? A toxic work environment has severe detrimental consequences. By toxic, I am referring to negative harsh bullying, and cruel behavior directed toward co-workers as with gossip, back-stabbing, humiliation, and mockery. Often times, it is directed toward those who do not seem to fit in, i.e., the quiet, reserved personalities, people less apt to converse in small talk, and those who focus on the tasks at hand. Quiet people may be more goal-oriented, not social. And when the quiet ones are ostracized, treated as different, a damaging scenario unfolds.

Children and adults need to be taught that negative behavior such as bullying and abuse of others, (i.e., relatives, friends, co-workers) will not be tolerated. Good behaviors ought to be modeled by parents, educators, religious and civic leaders, and supervisors, teaching not only by example, but also with words. There will be individuals in public spaces that are at various levels of emotional growth and may learn differently. This will have a bearing on social environments.

Good ethics and morality involves helping others feel valued by upholding their intrinsic worth by our thoughts, words, and deeds—the way we treat them. People can feel if they are valued by others or devalued, and it is our moral obligation to help others feel loved no matter how different they are from us. By God's grace we are forgiven, loved, and redeemed; as we have received let us in turn, extend that same grace to others. As an advisor said to me: "Ordinary human kindness goes a long way in making people's lives better, from day one."[10]

Along with healthy social interactions there are individual behaviors that contribute to a healthy spirituality. I have found certain daily habits to be helpful in my recovery process. The first thing I do every day when I drink my morning coffee is to read a Bible and other devotional literature. During this time I also pray and may listen to music. Without this daily ritual I would feel empty and lost. I also believe that the act of repentance plays a role in healing a person of mental illness. It is a very healthy practice to make an honest assessment of one's faults and shortcomings and say, "I'm sorry," to God; and along with that, repenting, by actually saying, "I repent," which is not complete without turning in the opposite direction and trying not to repeat the mistake. Sometimes I'm too critical of others so I work on being less judgmental and I ask God to help me to see the good in

---

10. Anonymous advisor, email message to author, January 10, 2018.

Civility, Grace, and Mental Health

others, to help me love as God loves. I pray, asking God to help me to forgive others, saying, "Please fill me with forgiveness for the ways I've been hurt or offended, and help me to treat others the way I want to be treated myself."

Most of all when I am feeling the heavy burden of despair, I remind myself that I am not permitted to think that God doesn't love me or care about what happens to me. Though as hard as it may seem at the time, I need to have faith that God is good and that God loves those he has created.

Medicine, *alone*, will not cure mental disorders. Psychotherapy, *alone*, will not cure behavior disorders. Love and support, *alone*, will not heal the broken hearted and those with mental problems. What we need in order to recover is fellowship in a religious community and prayer directed toward a higher power. I put my hope in God, and when I pray I know that God will hear me. Here is an example of what I often include in my supplications:

> *Almighty God*, Creator of heaven and earth, I praise you for you are holy. Thank you for all your goodness to me. I repent for all my sins, all the evil I have said and done in thoughts, words, and deeds. Please forgive me. I repent for things done and left undone. Please give me grace and faith. Fill me with the Holy Spirit—protect me from all evil, keep me safe. Lord Jesus, please expel any evil demons out of me and send them into the pigs. Cast them out and fill me with the Holy Spirit. Protect me. Let your Spirit surround me and keep me safe here, and as I go out of my home today. Let my spirit be one with yours and may your will be done—not mine. For you are God and I am not. Let me be a blessing to all I associate with. Give me a teachable heart, help me to learn, and grant me wisdom. Please help me with my loneliness. Lord, how can I know you better? Help me to hear you as you guide me. Give me clear guidance. Guide my leaders, too, in every area of my life. Help me to forgive those who hurt and abuse me. Bless them, my enemies; give them what they need. For you will not forgive me if I don't forgive others. Give me a humble heart full of humility; I do not want to be arrogant or proud or boastful. Teach me your ways.

Give me an undivided heart, meaning, and purpose for my life. Give me courage to deny myself and to take up my cross daily. Give me courage to face persecution and to always turn the other cheek; to never return evil for evil. Light my path and may all my work and life point only to you, giving glory to you and honor forever and ever. In Jesus Christ's holy and precious name I pray.

Amen and amen. Yes and yes.

* * *

How can those who have a mental illness find meaning in and purpose for their lives?

To be healthy and to find one's purpose in life, first of all, one needs two things: a vertical relationship with our maker who is God. And horizontally, good relationships in the form of friendships, co-workers, and family relations (whether by blood or spiritually, in the church). One cannot exist without the other for it has been said that in order to love God, one needs to also love one's neighbor which, hopefully, will be reciprocated. But what happens when the love of neighbor is not reciprocated? Then there is isolation. Sometimes we can break through the isolation by participating in a work environment. Work can be a purposeful activity; everyone needs something constructive to do on a daily basis. This often, for the mentally ill, may not mean 'competitive' employment—which is okay. By competitive I mean: able to work at the same speed and strength in hours, difficulties, complexities, etc., as the normate population. Non-competitive employment can include volunteer work in the church or community or work around the home, such as chores and finding projects to do. When volunteering in a public place it is helpful when the supervisor is willing to try to make things work for someone who has a disability by supporting their different needs.

I had an interesting experience volunteering in a hospital patient library. Toward the end of my time there I was dealing with multiple medical issues and I could not, on a physical or emotional level, perform my duties so I had to resign. But for twelve years I worked in the library, and though it had some challenges and was a lot of hard work, overall, it was a lot of fun and I felt needed. Part of my duties there was being the statistician and for my own edification I checked out and studied a college level course on statistics from the public library. I cannot emphasize enough the importance of education throughout one's entire lifetime. I have not only been aided by library resources but have been guided by mentors and personal instructors.

My work supervisor was extraordinary. She taught me new skills both in technology and socially, how to interact with others. She taught me how to be gutsy and how to take risks. She opened doors. My supervisor had great compassion for all her volunteers with disabilities or special needs, and went all out to help them feel included. She showed patience for my shortcomings, had a forgiving attitude, and tolerated my faults. By example and spoken word, she showed me and my co-workers how to respect one another and to value each other though we are all different in personality types, abilities, and talents. Even though she was fun loving, I was also deeply impressed by her strong work ethic and sacrificial attitude in the service of others: patients, staff and volunteers.

My supervisor, though imperfect, is a great example of how someone can be a good Christian leader in the secular workforce where we encounter a pluralistic environment with differing viewpoints and beliefs. She is an example of how the ethical lifestyle of Christianity has branched out into the world, and has been integrated into the secular workforce without compromising itself. I will always be grateful for all she did for me. She is an exemplary human being with character of the highest caliber, and I feel honored that I was able to spend twelve years under her supervision. I learned a great deal, and became a more well-rounded person for having known and worked for her. I can't say enough for how grateful I am to the institution that opened its doors to me and allowed me the privilege of working under her.

Spirituality can help define what is important to us in our everyday lives and the choices we make. Various lifestyles reflect our choices. I believe there is more to life than feeling good or nice all the time—but some choose to use drugs or alcohol to try to feel happy. I did not have a problem with this kind of behavior, myself, because my past experience with people who abused alcohol was very hurtful; I saw what alcohol does to people and how cruel they became toward me. The way they treated me when intoxicated was very unpleasant. Alcohol destroyed relationships. I now totally abstain from alcohol and keep a big distance between myself and those who drink.

However, many people with mental illness have chosen this path of substance abuse which more often than not, leads to self-destruction. Along with this kind of lifestyle comes sexual promiscuity which can lead to contracting sexually transmitted diseases which often leads to serious disability and/or death. Unhealthy habits, including smoking, and little mental stimulation can, and often does, bring physical and mental deterioration. Therefore one needs to abstain from these substances and eat healthy foods, read and do other types of activities to maintain and improve brain function. As a way to improve my mental abilities and everyday general function I read, often study chess, and classical Latin. Being socially engaged at least part of the day is imperative.

Meaning, purpose, and hope go together. When we value something, a project or activity that gives us a sense of purpose, it is therefore meaningful for us. If it is something others consider useful and they validate that it has importance, this gives us motivation and good esteem. Those who has been beaten down socially will need to find importance in their work and place of worship. Socially, teachers and friends can build up someone with a mental illness and encourage a positive sense of self, to help a person see a new, valued image of themselves—not overblown into conceit or egotism—but a balanced view of oneself that will acknowledge one's own weakness and strengths with compassion and patience for one's shortcomings.

A friend explained the importance of hope and how we find it: "To have hope is to have the belief that my life is worthwhile. God has put me on this earth and expects something out of me.

Civility, Grace, and Mental Health

There is a purpose in my being here and it is my job to figure it out. When I find a reason for my life I will gain hope."[11]

My steps to improvement in mental health have included: Finding a good church to attend and participate in; finding a mental health professional: psychiatrist, therapist, or counselor for medical and psychological treatments; finding social support in a religious setting, work environment or community/education activity, and sports/exercise activity.

My daily routine consisting of caring for physical, mental, and emotional health with good nutrition and physical exercise; education-brain stimulation/exercising the mind; loving relationships and social interaction. I try to maintain daily spiritual disciplines of scripture reading/study; prayer; meditation/listening for God's guidance and obtaining guidance from an advisor.

Throughout my lifetime I have often wondered why am I so sick and weak. I learned the answer to my own question: Sickness, weakness, and disability helps us to realize our dependence upon God. It can also deal with eliminating pride. An analogy would be when we get physically hurt, we turn to a physician; and when we are spiritually ill, we must turn to God, to seek His help. The Bible clearly says to turn to both, God and medicine—they work together.

I used to be physically attractive and I thought it was the most important way to find happiness. But then my mental illness led me to realize my dependence on God in the struggle against evil and answers in the supremacy of Jesus Christ. And as my disabilities increased in number, physically, emotionally, and mentally, I was being reminded that God is the source of life and health, personally, socially and otherwise. A remnant of pride still creeps up on me but I remind myself that God is the source of my competence. Without God, I›m nothing.

I mentioned this to an advisor and he answered, "Yes. I think the experience of being weak—of being inadequate to facing up to what is against you—is fundamental to all biblical piety. It›s Israel›s experience among the nations, it›s the repeated

11. Farraj, "Hope," In: *For Healing*, 11.

experience from which the Psalms cry out; 'Save me, O God, for the waters have come up to my neck' Ps. 69:1 ESV); it›s the experience of Christ on the cross (no one is more helpless than someone nailed fast to a tree); and the experience of Paul as a missionary: 'If I must boast, I will boast of the things that show my weakness,' 2 Cor. 11:30 (ESV)."[12]

My religious faith is what gives me hope and strength. It brings me comfort and healing through my connection with a higher power. If I get upset or angry, it helps prevent a violent reaction to my emotions and promotes a more peaceful resolution. Spirituality brings wholeness and helps me to be in touch with my true self. Spirituality helps me re-think what I value, what are my priorities and goals. When I experience suffering, my faith reminds me that there is more meaning to life than just nice feelings. Modern-day hedonism is a result of thinking we should always feel good and constantly experience pleasure, the flight from responsibility. The question is one of morals, ethics, and personal choices.

To help psychiatric in-patients with spiritual issues and to support their complex mental and emotional needs, I thought of another role I could perform in my volunteer position at the hospital which was to start a spiritual care support group on a unit—the first of its kind for this institution—under the guidance of my friend and former long-distance mentor, The Reverend Dr. Timothy H. Little. Reverend Little, a past pastor and chaplain, also happens to be visually impaired by blindness. His background consists of a doctorate of ministries in the Presbyterian denomination and chaplain supervisor position, last employed in the University of California Davis Medical Center in Sacramento. Now retired, he previously specialized in mental health and was also a spiritual counselor and therapist.

I sought for and obtained permission from the hospital administration to do the group, and along with cooperation with the Spiritual Services department who provided a chaplain, twice a month support sessions were held where religious areas of thought and spiritual needs were addressed. The groups were well attended

---

12. Anonymous advisor, email message to author, March 10, 2018

by patients of various age levels and backgrounds, as there appeared to be great interest. We held the gatherings in the unit's dining room, sitting at the tables. To begin, I shared with them who I was, a former psychiatric patient who is in recovery. This was a quiet, peaceful time period for the patients who were rather subdued and a bit shy, but they went along with our prompts, discussing what is important for themselves in the areas of their religious faith, values, feelings, and goals in their own personal healing, including their hopes and dreams for the future. It gave the patients an opportunity to speak out one at a time, knowing they'd be heard, which for many may not happen very often. During this time, they knew someone cared about them (in this case, a chaplain and a hospital volunteer and former patient) who wished to support their deepest needs.

Unfortunately, the chaplain I was working with left in retirement after a few months and to my great disappointment the Spiritual Services department would not provide a replacement. However, it was a good experience for me and the hospitalized patients while it existed, by the kind and nature of care it provided. It would be helpful for other hospitals and clinics around the country to follow suit because this is the type of program that greatly benefits the psychiatric patients in that it promotes their healing and recovery.

So spirituality is of paramount importance to psychiatric inpatients, as it has been in my own life journey. As a part of spirituality, my personal values and motivations will be reflected in my life choices—what the world sees. However, when I go through a period of depression my resolve is often weak.

My advisor further explained: "It comes down to love or desire, I suppose. That's how Augustine thinks of it. Love is motivation in that it is a motive force, like a force of attraction that pulls us toward what we love. So whatever we love to do, we are motivated to do, and we love paying attention to it, keeping at it. *Diligence* comes from a Latin word for love. The problem with depression or exhaustion is that it weakens the motive force of love.

But when we're healthy and well-rested, we're free to do what we love, and to love doing it."[13]

I responded: "The problem with that is people usually love all the wrong things and the wrong people. Sometimes it seems that nothing works out."

My advisor answered: "The problems with love come in two dimensions:

1. Disordered love, where you love things in the wrong order, loving lower things as if they were higher things, and vice versa (putting money above friendship, for example).

2. Diminished ability to love anything: a result of exhaustion, depression, or the vice that the Christian tradition calls by various names: sloth, acedia, tristitia (Aquinas's definition: 'sadness about the good,' where you see the good you should pursue but just don't care enough to pursue it—talk about lack of motivation!)

"*Disordered love* is essentially Augustine's definition of sin. Lots of people over the centuries have found it helpful in thinking about their moral lives."[14]

I often need to stop and ask myself, "What do I value in a spiritual life or when I am following my heart? As I reflect back, what has been my story, experiences? What important events shaped my spirit and life?

Upon reflection I can see that at times when I wandered from my religious faith, suffering and hardship brought me back to God—though not always immediately. Sometimes, I would flounder about for a time period, lost, and becoming increasingly mentally ill as I fell into a downward spiral. I would, however, eventually reach the realization that without God, I could not survive. So I'd go back to the church.

Had I lived a pampered, cushioned existence, my recent resolve to follow Christ may have been weaker. Hardship, then, I

---

13. Anonymous advisor, email message to author, January 10, 2018
14. Ibid.

believe, fashions the soul as exertion of our bodies will strengthen the muscles as in weight resistance training. How often do we come up against resistance only to be compelled all the more to assert ourselves? I have observed that when people rise from the worst adversity and combine that with faith, it can do the most good. Our hardships can also give us the empathy to help others in similar situations. Without empathy there is usually little compassion; maybe intellectual ascent to apply religious principles, but no compassion.

What is important in order for me to have a balanced life? For me, I need prayer and worship, spending time with others. I need to feel a sense of belonging. Where do I feel I belong? First of all, I need to feel that I have a right relationship with God. As I mentioned before about repentance, if there is some sin that needs to be confessed or some relationship issue that needs to be resolved, it is important to take care of this as far as it is within my ability. Much sorrow is the result of failing to repent of our sins. Much depression is a result of not bringing our shortcomings before God and asking for forgiveness; saying not only "I'm sorry," but voicing a deep heart-felt remorse for past wrongs. Much suicide could be prevented by bringing all our guilt feelings and sorrow about our faults or sinful actions to God in prayer, saying we were wrong and therefore, ask for forgiveness.

Psychology will fail without religion because some aspects of depression cannot be healed without repentance. When psychology acknowledges a higher power and how humans can find peace with God through repentance, then we will have an integration of psychology and spirituality.

Then there is social belonging and this consists of different levels. A few people know me well, some more at a distance and, sometimes, just being out in a public space I am among others. Here are some places where I have found friends: The workplace, social club, religious organization, organizations for education and higher learning, and recreational or sports participation.

There are certain words to think about that may be important for recovery. A therapist can ask someone who is in their care:

What does this word remind you of? What does it make you think of? Let's start with *forgiveness*.

Forgiveness brings me back to the history of my relationship with my mother. She has since passed away but I still remember how difficult it was for us to love each other. My father told me when I was an adult that my mother didn't want me. It is true I never felt wanted the entire time I was growing up and I confronted my mom in a letter when I was in my thirties. She replied that when she found out she was pregnant with me and told her mother, that her mother shouted at her in anger because my parents already had two toddlers in close range. It is understandable how difficult that would have been, especially since our family was of modest means. My mom said she was sorry I felt unloved and she didn't mean to be cruel.

I forgive her. I can understand the pressures she was under and her own psychological challenges. Toward the end of my mother's life she suffered from dementia. And this was a time when she very gently reached out to me in her infirmary, and expressed affection I had not known from her my entire life up to that point. I can honestly say that we made up and as her life ended, we truly loved one another. Forgiveness is to recognize hurt and go beyond it through reconciliation and remorse of both parties to finally reach the stage of healing. Which leads me to *peace*.

Peace is in knowing I am not angry or resentful toward anyone, including God. I have often been frustrated with my difficult life circumstances and have asked God to explain why these things happened to me: a challenging childhood, trauma-filled adulthood, and severe economic deprivation. But I learned that God doesn't have to answer to one of his creatures. I've come to accept that my understanding is limited and I need to continue to do the best I can with whatever resources are given to me. The church, the body of Christ, has been helpful when I was in a freefall; and I have come to believe that God is our only hope. *For it is by grace you have been saved, through faith—and this is not from yourselves, it is the gift of God—not by works, so that no one can boast.* (Eph. 2:8–9 NIV)

Additionally, in regard to the concept of *hope*, I asked my advisor to respond to my question of why, when there is so much injustice and suffering in the world, why should we still believe in the biblical claims of a loving God? At one point as I looked around me, I felt that the Bible was full of broken promises and wishful thinking: *Defends the poor*— doesn't happen all the time! *Frees the oppressed*—some, but not much! *Brings justice*—not around here! *Heals the sick*—Maybe, a precious few! *The church is Christ's body*—Then why are so many Christians apathetic about the needs of others?

My advisor responded: "It would be nice if it were that simple, as if we always saw God defending the poor and needy and afflicted. But then there would be no poor and needy and afflicted, and there would never have been Christ crucified. So I think that scenario would be a refutation of Christianity. To take the bad things we see happening as evidence against the God of the cross is simply a mistake. The truth is that Christian faith means living in hope for what we don't see happening around us, hope for a future that we can't see. For as Paul says, *hope that is seen is not hope* (Rom. 8:24 ESV). This is good news. If seeing bad things really were a refutation of Christianity, then our only reasonable option would be to despair. Evil wins. Only hope can say otherwise."[15]

Joy is a complicated emotion. Sometimes I think that just having my basic needs met brings me joy, if I have enough food, clothing, and shelter—what is essential. I have a circle of friends varying in degree of closeness, so that helps. I have been partially included in a religious community, and this is important for happiness. But the feeling of joy is elusive, especially when I have coped with clinical depression for most of my life. There were events that happened early on and into adulthood. For this story, please see my earlier memoir, *Voices in the Rain: Meaning in Psychosis*. The trauma has not been easily forgotten or overcome. Memories of the past still haunt me. Thus, the emotional baggage is very heavy and difficult to carry.

---

15. Anonymous advisor, email message to author, January 26, 2018.

I have asked God for feelings of joy and he periodically has answered my prayers. Often it comes in the small things: pleasant music, a good book, or a cup of coffee with a friend. And once in while I can laugh though this is infrequent. Again, I must say that it is in the worship of God in a religious service that meaningful emotions come to me, sometimes resulting in joy.

Love. We are to love people *in God*.[16] What does that mean? Our love should be wanting what is best for the person, to see them as God would see them and to have a purity of heart. It is not demanding or self-centered. It is to show restraint and be civil in social interactions. To always keep in mind that people are not our possessions, not those we should try to dominate or have control over. But to love as to build them up, not tear them down but to be a positive life force to strengthen someone in their times of need. Love is to celebrate the victories of life with a friend and to show support in times of grief. To be there as a listening ear, to listen well, and deeply to more than what spoken language conveys, for love is a language of the heart.

To promote healing and recovery a therapist can ask a patient: *What gives you strength to get through the day? What do you think about?* I, personally, remind myself that the suffering in this world is only temporary. Our real home is in heaven. I remember that periodically I find joy in life so I can look forward to that again. My ministry work needs to be done and that is why I was born and I need to persevere. I try to find strength by reading scripture and other supportive materials. I pray for strength and also try to find supportive friends to talk with.

The therapist can ask: *What has inspired you? Tell me about something that inspired you—a person or something that happened.* For me, the study of historical people has inspired me. Seeing their examples, motivations, and achievements help me to feel that big obstacles can be overcome; mountains can be moved.

Along with the previously mentioned questions a therapist can have their clients reflect on the following: *What do you see as your talents and gifts?* For example, what was your favorite subject

---

16. Cary, "Augustine," Teaching Company.

or activity in school? What were you good at? What are you good at now? Do you play a musical instrument? Do you read books? What kind of books do you enjoy reading? Do you enjoy writing? What kind of things do you write about? If you could have any kind of job you wanted, what kind of work would you enjoy doing?

A therapist can ask about a higher power: *If you could ask your higher power just one question, and you knew you would get an answer, what would that one question be?* In addition, what will spark the patient's *creativity*, as well as the more important task of how to find answers to the question of *meaning*?

What is the way I, personally, find deep meaning in my life? Or what do I find meaningful? Worshipping God in a church on Sunday mornings has been one of the most meaningful activities of my life, especially, a Roman Catholic mass. At one point, in my thirties, I even joined a Roman Catholic church. But because I lacked a vehicle, which meant that I could not reach the church to worship on Sundays, I went to another church nearby which I could walk to. The great depth, beauty, and formality of a Catholic mass feeds my soul. My heart yearns to someday hear a mass done in classical Latin, an ancient language I, myself, have studied.

Saint Augustine, an early church father, is a very interesting historical figure for me. I would like to read his *City of God* in classical Latin. I would like to speak and pray in Latin. I know that during Martin Luther's time of the Protestant Reformation (1517)[17] there were some problems regarding the ways of the Roman Catholic Church, but we need to try to understand each other and forgive, going forward to seek unity as one Universal church— for I believe that all Christians are the body of Christ.

I am conservative in my theological beliefs but I am liberal in my social acceptance, tolerance, and inclusion of others. So I am both, conservative and liberal. I find the church, in general, to be made up of many high quality human beings. I've met Christians who are working tirelessly to free the oppressed in a broken criminal justice system. There are some who work at food pantries, help with disaster relief, and serve the poor in many ways too numerous

17. Bainton, *Here I Stand*, 60–64.

to list here, all to build a more robust and whole society. Christians improve just about every sector of our culture for the greater good, or at least they have that potential.

I long to know God in still deeper ways. And I want to serve the poor. I find meaning in knowing that my existence has a purpose. The purpose of my life besides worshipping God, is taking part in the ministry work the Lord gave me to do which is to serve people of all economic levels who have a mental illness.

To help a person with mental illness to grow in wisdom and to recover, a therapist can further ask: *What have you learned about life from this painful experience of mental illness? And how did the crisis you go through relate to your personal faith? Were your religious beliefs a help in handling this rough situation? Do you see anything constructive resulting from coping with this difficult experience? Does all this seem to have any meaning as you understand things? What is the meaning as you interpret it?*[18]

To direct a person in their care, a therapist can help by directing thoughts in a certain direction to increase motivation. Such questions as: *What values do you claim as the most exciting and that really make life worth living? When do you feel most alive (hopeful, like celebrating the goodness of life) or feel the most zest for life? When do you have the most and then the least amount of energy?*[19]

Personally, my workday life has the most hope, energy, and motivation when my mind is engaged in a project. Often, I've felt that focusing on God and contemplating abstract theological concepts are what bring me the most joy though I know that God loves people, too—so I also need to engage socially to be healthy.

I feel the least energy and joy when I have self-centered or negative thoughts. I have learned that an access of self-absorption can lead to mental illness. There is a danger when someone feels rejected by others, because then a person can over-compensate and just turn inward, thinking only about themselves, and their own needs. They may live in isolation. When I attended a

---

18. Clinebell, *Counseling for Spiritually Empowered Wholeness*, 90–93.
19. Ibid.

women's Bible study many years ago we used to say: S–I–N, the "I" is in the center. Yet, a person can also be all alone at times and focus their thoughts outwardly on other people and work, and this can be healthy.

Someone who has a mental illness can ask themselves: *What are the parts of my faith that enrich my relationships? What are the parts of my faith that help me handle losses and what do I do to strengthen and deepen my spiritual life?*[20] Answers to these questions are key to recovery. Of all the people I know who experience a mental illness disability, the ones who are believers in God and participate in a religious community are the most successful socially, and in their everyday lives. And it is my guess that more suicides are done by atheists and those who've rejected God; for then where can one find hope without a greater power and the promises in scripture?

So, yes, mental health is about how we treat others and how we, ourselves, are treated, in family relationships, the religious community, the workplace, schools, and other public spaces. How people cope and adjust to mistreatment will depend on resiliency; but it can also result in suffering a breakdown and mental malady. The distress from destructive interactions take their toll in emotional and/or physical violence in the home, workplace absenteeism and loss of productivity to our economy, schools' high drop-out rate, and crime and homelessness on the streets.

Simple acts of kindness have the power to prevent injury and can heal the wounded. Simple acts of kindness everyday have the power to strengthen our children. Simple acts of kindness can thus build a greater society.

While it is true that much of the hurt in our world comes as a result of what religion refers to as original sin and depravity within humans, much can be avoided through moral education and the power of example or role models. When children can see the right way to treat and interact with others, there is more hope for their own behavior to be just and right.

---

20. Ibid.

To Loose the Bonds of Injustice

Forgiveness, as a constant practice, is also a key to building a more just and right society. This is true regardless of which religious tradition one has or even for a nonbeliever. Learning patience and forgiving one another *without retaliation* goes a long way in promoting a healthier society where emotional injuries are lessened and there is less likelihood in increasing mental problems. Christ died on the cross, taking the most mistreatment of all to make the world not only a better place through his absorption of evil. He died and was resurrected to simultaneously resurrect a dying world, battered and torn by the destruction of hate, cruelty, and violence. It is by his suffering that we are healed, and this new life—living in God's love—is for everyone, including the mentally ill. And who are we to question him?

Chapter 4

Cultural Expectations and Christian Identity

A person is mentally healthy to the degree that he is able to live the two great commandments, to love God and neighbor fully.[1]

CHARLIE SWIFTLY SLAMMED THE door closed. Or attempted to—as two male police officers in black pushed their way into his apartment, shoving him against the wall.

"What are you doing?!" Charlie frantically cried out, shouting angry expletives.

"Just calm down—put your hands behind your back!" the tall muscular officer barked.

As the policeman snapped handcuffs around his wrists, Charlie squirmed, trying to get away. His small red-haired cocker spaniel, Tippy, ran up yelping unendingly. Turning his face, Charlie tried to sooth Tippy with comforting words.

"We're taking you to the ER," the short, stocky officer said. "We know you had plans to kill yourself—you need help."

Charlie realized then that a person doesn't close a door on policemen. They will win. Earlier he had been on the phone with a friend; and, yes, he had told his friend that he planned to jump off the Iowa Avenue bridge to his death. Charlie didn't know how to swim and since he was severely over-weight he was sure it was going to be successful. His voices had been tormenting him day and

1. Clinebell Jr, "Mental Health Through the Religious Community," 34.

night, saying he should break into a house located down the street, a small single-story cottage-type structure occupied by an elderly woman with several disabilities that weakened her. Charlie's voices said she was an easy target. The constant voices were tormenting him, causing extreme emotional turmoil.

The police officers pushed Charlie into the back of the squad car but it wasn't easy as Charlie struggled violently. The back seat was bare of cushions, hard, with just a board, and it was hot. Being July, the car needed air conditioning, and he felt stifled in the steamy heat but no cool air reached him. The drive took ten minutes and soon Charlie was seated in an exam room as a physician assistant took control. The friend who had alerted the police of Charlie's suicide plan was also there. And a counselor from Hillcrest, a support for daily living staff person under whose care Charlie had been receiving guidance, arrived within an hour. Hillcrest Supportive Living provides assistance for those in need of developing skills regarding practical activities such as grocery shopping, home maintenance, and goal setting.[2]

Charlie was evaluated by medical personnel and released. He promised to follow-up with his therapist in a couple of days, a clinical social worker specializing in psychiatry whom he regularly saw once a month. Charlie made a verbal contract with the medical staff to not harm himself and to seek diversions of his psychological pain by spending time with his friends. He was alone too much and isolated, they thought. The medical staff also increased the dose of his anti-psychotic medication. In the end, Charlie felt humiliated and traumatized by the hospital visit and went home to take care of his dog, his only solace.

* * *

The diverse opinions of what reality consists of or worldviews have important implications for psychiatry in Western culture, as well as around the world. Treatment options are based on how psychiatry views reality. There are healthcare providers who periodically

---

2. Anonymous person in communication with author, May 28, 2018.

assert what they believe is helpful in treatment options; but, unfortunately, powerful business interests often dominate the field of psychiatry with profit goals as we see in pharmaceutical giants putting pressure on researchers to bring about certain favorable results. I'm not against psychiatric medications, they have their place; however, there ought to be a balance in how often or in what quantity they are administered within an overall holistic treatment plan. It is when medications are promoted as the sole, absolute, cure-all that we run into problems.

It is significant that the dogmatism of cultures contain within themselves various subgroups each with their own perspectives within not only religion, where we commonly hear the term "dogma;" there is also the dogmatism of science with theoretical paradigms reaching even into popular culture. Once we believed the world was flat and that the earth was the center of the known universe. With the acquiring of new knowledge comes the shifting of paradigms, one coming to the fore, only to recede shortly thereafter.

Within Western mainstream psychiatry—a branch of scientific medicine—the dominate focus is on a physical cause of mental disorder and thus, medications are administered with great enthusiasm. This theory of a broken brain is based on a certain materialist worldview; however, on a worldwide scale it is important to acknowledge that there are various interpretations and diverse models of illness within different cultures. I would add that the diverse models do not always represent a contradiction or cancel each other out, but may often represent complimentary aspects of a single phenomenon.

As various scientific perspectives inevitably have come into vogue this has resulted in a change of perspective of what constitutes reality, especially when what constitutes fundamental foundational structures has changed. One such example would be in the field of quantum physics, theory, and mechanics.[3] The metaphysical questions resulting from quantum theory has subsequent implications for psychiatric research and for the care and

3. Kaiser, *How the Hippies*, xxiv.

treatment of the mentally ill. Cultural-political factors of great impact influenced the direction of science in the first half of the 1900s in Europe and the United States when philosophical questions in physics— and science in general—were curtailed in favor of a pragmatic approach [pragmatism][4] which amounted to not asking questions and just focusing on calculations. And because of this, modern psychiatry, as a branch of science, has largely evolved as a pragmatic, materialist science with philosophical questions and schools of thought such as existentialism shunned or prevented from being explored.[5]

If such inquiries are to be given legitimacy what, then, would be the implications of Bell's theorem,[6] (including quantum entanglement and nonlocality[7]), both metaphysically and philosophically, in regard to the nature of reality?[8] —for how we experience the world and, subsequently, how we interpret all aspects of human nature including our relationship with God? How can we know God?

As you probably are already aware there are at minimum two camps, and the question of quantum non-locality and entanglements in Bell's theorem is ample evidence that Newtonian mechanistic physics has been challenged and I would say superseded by the view of an uncertain and unpredictable material universe. Though research has developed a mathematically precise paradigm on the quantum level, how one can relate this to the macroscopic level has been a constant challenge.[9] For on the one hand, we have precise mathematical descriptions of quantum phenomena; but how to make sense of this in terms that are familiar from our macroscopic, human-sized experiences has so far perplexed theorists and researchers alike. As David Kaiser, Germeshausen

---

4. Ibid., 43.

5. Anonymous psychiatric professional, email message to author, January 1999.

6. Ibid., 36–37.

7. Ibid.

8. Ibid., xxiv.

9. Kaiser, email message to author, Mary 27, 2018.

Professor of the History of Science and Professor of Physics at the Massachusetts Institute of Technology has noted:

> "We have exquisitely precise mathematical descriptions of quantum phenomena such as quantum entanglement. The challenge is to make sense of the mathematics (and the corresponding experimental data) in terms that are familiar from our macroscopic, human-sized experiences. But that continuing question of interpretation is rather distinct from having a "mathematically precise paradigm" for such effects, which we certainly do possess."[10]

Whatever its current stance, the changing dominant scientific views will continue to influence the direction of psychiatry. And in this power struggle of perspectives various competing authorities wish to define the terms. It has been the rule that whoever has the most power usually defines the terms in both academic and political arenas; however, the way *power* is defined is, itself, questionable. Which leads us to the pressing questions of how mind, mental illness, recovery, and cure will be defined and based on what criteria? And what, then, will be subsequent options for treatment? Various perspectives of reality with its consequential epistemologies will produce specific fruit in psychiatric practice for good or for ill, as newly emerging theorists and researchers continue the debate.

Along with quantum physics and its indeterminate view of cause and effect, and the question of relationships reaching from within micro-scopic levels into the macro-scopic, a relatively new field has emerged called transpersonal psychology which seeks to integrate the mind and body with the immaterial spirit.[11] This perspective offers to transcend a physical mindset with what it purports to be a higher purpose and to reach for a greater potential in life than mere physical survival. To find such purpose this psychology builds on things such as religious values and beliefs with an acknowledgement of a higher power from which our livelihood

---

10. Ibid.
11. Free Dictionary, "Transpersonal Psychology," lines 1-2.

depends. God, then, for many, becomes the focus of one's life in contrast to accumulating wealth or other materialistic goals.

Once the spiritual aspect of the human is granted and all that entails, we seek to understand the world around us in light of this notion. It is at this point that the value system of good and evil on a spiritual level becomes apparent and reality, then, consists of good and evil forces. Humans—consisting of body, mind, and spirit—can reflect both good and evil or some of each, at different times and by various degrees. For a person whose body is sick, they seek healing. And, likewise, with a person's mind and spirit that has fallen ill, there is the need for them to be made right again spiritually. Psychiatry needs to acknowledge that human mind and the interconnected spirit can go bad or become ill—by various degrees—and that this is a spiritual problem corrected by a value system that has its origin in a spiritual paradigm. A diseased tree will not bear healthy fruit. In the United States, a new label for psychiatric care is *Behavioral Health,* which carries the implication that patients' spiritual health or illness, as reflected by behaviors, need to be addressed accordingly.

As a Christian and person in recovery from a mental illness, I believe the sole aim of humans is to know God and to live in such a way as to bring glory to God. Any lifestyle contrary to this pattern will produce diseased fruit as from a diseased tree. From my religious perspective, this also opens ourselves up to evil forces bent on our destruction. Mental illness is the destruction of a person and a sickness of the soul. Fighting against such destruction can, and often is, a daily battle and some people with mental illness succumb to defeat. Medications have their place but do not address the sickness of the soul. That is why we need God who, alone, has authority over sickness and death. I know, personally, that without God, I cannot survive.

So, yes, scientific perspectives matter. Individual worldviews of psychiatrists are important and influence the quality of care for the mentally ill. And the perspectives patients live with will determine the quality of their lives. Anyone who denies this doesn't realize the high stakes involved and severe consequences for such denial. For good or for ill, the choices we make will not only determine the outcomes of our own lives, but will have consequences in the lives of others. And when a psychiatrist neglects the spiritual aspects of the mentally ill or fails to support a patient's choice in a religious lifestyle, I maintain that little success toward recovery will follow. Patients need more than a pill. The pharmaceutical company is not God. I don't know all the answers and though I believe that psychiatric drugs may have a place in the treatment plan, they do not supersede the spiritual aspect of recovery which, alone, belongs to a higher power. The spiritual aspect of the psychiatric patient must not be a neglected component of the recovery model. It can be a matter of life and death.

This leads us to differing viewpoints of reality as described by people of various cultures. It is beyond the scope of this present work to sum up the differences in cultural perspectives in all parts of the world outside the United States, e.g., U.K. and Europe, South American countries, Asia and Africa. Mental illness is much more complex than at first glance. I will provide a limited amount of examples found in the previously mentioned book (see chapter 3), *Our Most Troubling Madness*. One thing to consider: Is there a common denominator that defies cultural norms, a universal cause in this mental condition and would there be a universal remedy or recovery model?

Luhrmann and Marrow maintain that the Western response to schizophrenia is harsh and psychologically crushing for those with psychiatric diagnoses. That for the individual who receives a diagnoses of *schizophrenia*, this is like receiving a death sentence.[12] The person can no longer find employment, housing, or food—provide for themselves at the most basic level. In addition, on the social level, they are thrown to the bottom of society, rejected, and treated as less than human which the authors call *social defeat*.[13]

This book proposes a more favorable view of practices in developing nations which—the contributors claim—show healthier outcomes. I find this questionable from my viewpoint as one in the

12. Luhrmann and Marrow, *Our Most Troubling Madness*, 104.
13. Ibid., 25.

recovery process who lives in a Western culture. I find fault with the idea that the approach of developing nations is superior. For example, this view makes light of the fact that in the peasant class in India, the male spouse may physically harm or take the life his wife usually with no legal repercussions. The writers say that the mentally ill wife in India, if she is still able to fulfill her domestic role in the family she will be supported. In their case examples, the wife in the peasant class does not work outside the home, so if she can mind children, sweep the floors, wash the clothes, dishes, and cook, then there is some acceptance. However, she may still be physically harmed for any infraction of the husband's moody judgements, and she, being aware of this situation, undoubtedly experiences significant emotional distress which most likely will exacerbate psychiatric symptoms.

The contributors of this book claim that in some developing countries a mentally ill family member who is chained to a log is better off simply by being within close proximity to his relatives.[14] This is absurd. Anything involving chains is extreme and inhumane. I appreciate, though, how difficult a situation can be if a mentally ill family member is violent and dangerous. How to solve such problems in this situation needs greater development.

Because of the previous examples, I disagree with the premise of this book and see independent living for the mentally ill person in the West as preferable to the problems in a close-knit family unit in a developing nation. Admittably, social isolation can be and often is a negative consequence of Western culture which can lead to self-destructive behaviors, as well as possible sociopathic ones. Then how a person sees the purpose in life and how to fulfill ones social and work-related goals will be a factor in isolation. Where do we find friends? Where do we belong? And how do we form friendships given problems of stigmatization?

The account of a Romanian woman in *Our Most Troubling Madness*, is telling of the state of psychiatry in that region and options for survival.[15] As an unwed parent who is forced to live with

14. Ibid., 8.
15. Ibid., 139–47.

Cultural Expectations and Christian Identity

her elderly mother, just trying to survive occupies their entire day. After a brief stint doing factory work in a neighboring city, she returns to her hometown, psychotic, only to be shunned by the town's people. Her mother keeps a garden and the few foods produced barely ward off starvation. The woman passes in and out of psychotic episodes, and is hospitalized.[16]

During one of the periods living out of this institution the woman is welcomed into an Evangelical community, United States missionaries. They teach her what she did not hear from her Orthodox priest whom she initially consulted, that God loves her unconditionally and without limit.[17] This joyful news fills her with an abundance of hope. Her Romanian psychiatrist sees her constant reference to Jesus Christ, the Holy Spirit, and God the Father, as further evidence of mental derangement[18]; however, he acquiesces in the end by providing her a stable environment to live in—the institution, itself. The missionaries provide for her: they take care of her son, bring her clothing, food, and companionship. Though the Orthodox priest blamed her for what he referred to as the sin of mental illness,[19] her Evangelical community gives her nonjudgmental, loving support. The psychiatrist, himself of Orthodox background, learns to tolerate what he sees as her "psychotic" behavior: constant joy, happiness, and new-found identity as a child of God.[20]

The way people view the world and how they see their place in it, what is their role and responsibility, will heavily influence a recovery outcome. Along with these perspectives a harsh economic reality steps in: how can we obtain food, clothing, and shelter? Who will hire a person with a mental illness diagnosis? And who will pay a living wage? Many people with mental illness in both the West and developing countries, whether in recovery or not, live the life of a pauper, a beggar. When a person comes from a family

16. Ibid., 142–43
17. Ibid., 149–50.
18. Ibid., 148
19. Ibid.
20. Ibid., 151–52

that has a toxic social environment, one of the main causes for the person's mental illness in the first place, removal from the unit is the only healthy option. That is when community programs and federal benefits come into play which, unfortunately, only provide scant support and which are so meager that a person trying to live on them can barely survive.

In addition, a serious issue is that many of the mentally ill who are abused are doubly stigmatized and victimized because no one will believe them when they report that they have been mistreated. Mentally disabled people are much more likely to be mistreated than the non-disabled population because they are thought of as weak, dependent, and definitely more vulnerable. No one expects them to defend themselves. Everything is blamed on their mental illness, i.e., that they are purportedly *delusional*. The person has to stand up for themselves, but often this is not adequate. Perpetrators of bullying often get away with their mistreatment. They can commit emotional and physical violence because they use the victim's alleged *mental condition* as a defense. Countless children, spouses, church members, employees, etc., are disbelieved when they report abuse and they have no one to defend or advocate for them.

The mental health industry needs to train advocates to stand up for the vulnerable, especially those who are at the bottom of power structures. People who have lower status in all organizations need advocates who will believe their stories of mistreatment and who will stand up for them—possibly helping them, if necessary, to leave the abusive situations and institutions. Currently, there is some advocacy: mental health workers and social workers will place a child under foster care.

Churches are not exempt. People in power (or who erroneously assume they have power) can mistreat church members and try to get away with it. We need to hold pastors and other church leaders accountable for their actions. As the saying goes: *Absolute power corrupts absolutely.* No one should be given a free reign in religious, educational, or workplace situations. Treating others with dignity and respect must be held up to high standards and the people in positions of leadership need to be held accountable.

Cultural Expectations and Christian Identity

On the flip side, a healthy organization will use conflict resolution processes to heal an interruption in the harmonious balance of relationships. When conflict arises (an inevitable scenario due to our fallen nature) healthy pastors and other church leaders will encourage meeting together to discuss differences or misunderstandings. For a person who has emotional or social challenges, this is quite valuable because they may suffer from more disruptions of personality than the average person. Kind, compassionate leaders will extend an invitation to meet together to talk about what is going on and will be able to iron out difficulties.

Relational conflicts are bound to occur and it is a healthy practice to take a step back to think about how to mend those conflicts. Keeping open communication lines are important because once lines are broken there is no opportunity to heal relationships. The church is to be an entanglement of loving relationships, more mysterious than given credit, and when one member is estranged, the whole body of believers suffer.

The church culture is an organic body within our larger political cultures of the state and nation that the church may or may not reflect. As you are probably aware, these political cultures vary greatly across the United States and coincide with socioeconomic levels along with educational opportunities. In *Our Most Troubling Madness*, we need to compare cultural differences within their case studies and take into account the different socioeconomic levels as well as education. Some of their people do not place as much value on educational achievement, so it is difficult to make comparisons regarding the health quality of lifestyles.

Our Most Troubling Madness makes an unfair broad generalization about people in the US with schizophrenia and paints a dire picture. As I mentioned before, the contributors claim that in the United States, the label of *schizophrenia* is the closest thing to a death sentence because people are rejected for employment and socially—cannot find housing, food, or other means to survive. People who are told they are mentally ill are treated as though they are incompetent and worthless members of society, useless. And this constant twenty-four hour daily grind of insults and inhumane treatment which is experienced during a multitude of social interactions has the effect of crushing the emotions leading to despair and hopelessness. It is no wonder that five out of ten people with schizophrenia attempt suicide and one in ten succeeds.[21] This is yet another reason why the Christian people have an important role to eliminate stigma, promoting social justice in upholding the dignity and rights of this afflicted population.

One person who bravely exemplifies stoic determination to survive in the face of great obstacles is Teresa. Teresa grew up on a farm and became mentally ill in her early twenties. In the process of being born she received brain damage and also suffers from a mild form of cerebral palsy, a condition that affects her ability to walk. Many people who meet her may consider her intellectually disabled but she is quick to share that she completed four years in a Bible college and in our conversations she reveals intelligence.

Teresa obtains her identity from her religious faith. She cleans a Four Square church she is a member of several days a week and attends Sunday and Thursday worship. Her church friends see that at least some of her needs are taken care of, including driving Teresa once or twice a month to see her elderly mother. Teresa's mother phones her and writes on a regular basis. Her mother also provides canned goods which supplement Teresa's food budget. Teresa loves to shop and chooses the brightest, most colorful clothing items available. Besides working hard at her church, she spends a lot of time cleaning her apartment. Physically, she is very strong, but emotionally is very fragile though kind and generous. She reads the Bible daily and prays. One of her favorite past times is to read an old history book from the eighth grade.

Teresa has faced rejection from the mainstream of society and without her church she would have no social contact at all except for her mother. But she immediately forgives all who are cruel and uncaring and has advised me that, "We must forgive."

Some people have made great strides in overcoming obstacles that their catastrophic schizophrenic diagnosis usually creates.

21. Anonymous psychiatric professional, email message to author, November 7, 2011.

Cultural Expectations and Christian Identity

One woman I know of who is a Christian has worked full-time as a secretary for most of her adult life even though she went through some psychotic episodes early on. She donates blood on a regular basis to help sustain the life of an AIDs patient and told me her primary identity is in being a *child of God*.

There is a man who has supported himself in various capacities and finds fulfillment in his religious faith, in being an uncle, and doing photography. Still, another man worked as a volunteer in a healthcare setting until the same organization hired him part-time. He also has a religious faith and is active in his church. Another woman who has a mental illness has found fulfillment in being a wife, mother, and women's church leader. She shared that she had a loving, supportive family when growing up and also currently has a supportive spouse.

Of my examples of some who have a mental illness and who have in some fashion carved out a fulfilling life for themselves, most have a religious faith and are connected to a religious organization. Even, Richard, whom I mentioned earlier said about himself: "I am a Christian." Maybe that explains his quiet, nonviolent nature, and gratitude to the community he felt supported by.

Len, whom I mentioned in chapter two, is a person that finds his identity in three ways: religious faith, work, and his sense of obligation in caring for others. In our frequent interactions there has been very little mention of schizophrenia. He has a strong work ethic. He is quick to defend himself, his rights and dignity; and yet, is compliant in the system, humbly respecting the government officials who run the disability programs that sustain him, as well as the physicians, and counselors who take care of his physical and mental health needs. His is not a wasted life. Not only has he tried to fill his days with meaningful work, it is evident that in his prayers of intercession for those who frequent the Ped Mall and elsewhere, he shows a deep concern for the spiritual life and destinies of strangers.

How we are treated by those we encounter in society on a day to day basis has a great bearing upon our self-image and self-esteem. Critical looks, an accusing, judgmental tone of voice, or negative body language tells us what people think of us—there is no way to avoid it. And when people are unjustly accused of wrong doing, this hurts. For example, those who have a mental illness are often victimized in disputes with police for no fault of their own. Something similar to this almost happened to me.

Once, I was shopping in a neighborhood store, a well-known chain with a pharmacy, when an employee started darting around the aisles watching and following me. Minding my own business, I went to a couple of shelves and picked up what I needed. The employee appeared very nervous and fidgety. After a few minutes I walked up to the check-out counter and purchased my items. The same employee was at the register and by now looked extremely anxious. After he handed the bag to me I turned and walked toward the exit just as a police officer entered. I nodded and smiled at the officer as he walked past.

Upon reflection I am certain the employee had phoned the police and reported an alleged shoplifter. The way he had been acting I am sure his attention was centered on me. I am guessing that perhaps my low-income appearance caused discrimination. My old, worn, and tattered brown denim jacket gave off the appearance of someone poor, and maybe in some other way I looked like a marginalized person, definitely not middle-class. Whatever the reason, I ended up with a close encounter with the law. And had I not brought my items up to the register and paid for them at that exact moment I could have been wrongfully arrested for an alleged crime, held in jail, and prosecuted for a crime I didn't commit. In addition, this would have been posted in our local newspaper so my reputation would have been tarnished.

Things like this happen to other low-income and mentally ill people unjustly condemned by the courts. All it takes is to look a little different than the norm and we are pounced on by the proprietors of businesses. And the tragedy is, now the poor have even less access to legal representation because of legislative cuts in the judiciary system leaving the mentally ill without a proper defense and a competent lawyer to argue for them. As a result we have jails and prisons with a disproportionate amount of innocent low-income people whose rights are being trampled because of a lack of tolerance for people who look different or who come from a less privileged background. What we need is more tolerance of differences and less judgmentalism. What is tolerance? *Tolerance is respecting the dignity and rights of all persons, even those whose beliefs and behaviors differ from our own.*[22]

In contrast to the harsh social environment of some businesses, for me, libraries have always been places of welcome. Thought not perfect, most library staff will treat patrons in a respectful manner. Ever since I was a child I've enjoyed being around a lot of books and have benefited from the stillness of the milieu. One reason I've sought refuge in libraries is because during the time I was growing up my home resembled a battle ground, with fighting, violence (emotional and physical) and constant turmoil. On a couple of occasions I resorted to cutting my wrists and once overdosed on an entire bottle of adult Bayer aspirin.

There was never a moment's peace. So it was only natural to seek refuge in a quiet, peaceful place where I could obtain some emotional stability. I have immense gratitude to all the libraries and librarians who open their doors freely to anyone searching for knowledge, beauty, and truth. Libraries have, for me, been sanctums of tranquility and tremendous pleasure. From the lone chair in the space by the sunlit windows, to the multitude of stacks, thousands of books authored by lovers of the language arts created by innumerable publishers, presses, and editors all for the edification of readers.

Our great country, whatever its faults or shortcomings, should be recognized as a vast place of opportunity because of the open door policies of libraries, accessible for anyone, no matter what gender, race, ethnicity or economic level. Such opportunities can help make life more worthwhile, especially for those who face innumerable obstacles in life. God bless the libraries and the helpful people who work in them.

Previously, I mentioned my volunteer work in a hospital library. Part of my duties that helped me in my formation of a new

---

22. Borba, *Building Moral Intelligence*, 8.

positive self-image was to bring books and magazines to the psychiatric units. At one such unit the nurse manager arranged for my badge to be recognized to gain free access to the unit, just like a regular employee. So just like a paid staff person, I could come and go at will. This privilege helped my self-esteem. I felt good about myself. This formed in me a new identity as one who was competent and trusted by important others. This also led to my writing of small grants or funding requests to obtain needed items for the patients on this particular unit as well as others. We got storage cabinets, a player-piano, exercise machines, a stationary bike, games, disc players, music CDs, and other items.

Another part of my volunteering has involved the procurement of clothes for the psychiatric in-patients at the hospital. After first obtaining permission from the chair of the department, I held clothing drives at my church which resulted in an abundance of provisions. Then, the nursing staff at the units requested sweatpants for the patients as they were more comfortable for the use in the hospital which the patients were welcome to keep upon release. Many church members have been involved, from donating, to providing transportation to the hospital and also in helping me carry the bags of clothing to the units. I am very grateful for their generous help.

Near the end of my time of volunteering at the hospital in which I had accumulated over 5,000 hours of service, the psychiatric administration put together a luncheon in my honor and a tour of the outdoor patio off the children's psychiatric in-patient unit. Patio furniture had been purchased with the total hours of funding I had accumulated and they put a plaque with my name on the wall in the patio designating my work at the hospital. This contributed to my sense of healthy pride and accomplishment, while at the same time a feeling that I had been able to do some good in helping others with a mental illness. But most of all, with my identity as a child of God, this was all done for the glory of God, soli deo gloria!

* * *

Cultural Expectations and Christian Identity

On the flip side of overt prejudice against disabled human beings, their social rejection and subsequent isolation, is an inclusive community model called L'Arche, a place where everyone belongs. The most discriminated against people in the world are those with intellectual disabilities many of which also suffer from a mental illness. For a study in compassion, L'Arche is an international organization based on community support in group homes.[23]

Jean Vanier, founder of L'Arche, began this movement in 1964 to help those with a mental handicap feel respected and valued. Though currently affected by government intervention with rules and regulations, in its early history Vanier created a radical space for the outcasts of society to feel welcome in a violent and hurtful world. He also felt that we, the normates, had much to learn from those with intellectual disabilities in the matters of the heart.[24] Vanier's depth of compassion for those afflicted with mental, emotional, and spiritual challenges is beyond comparison. We would do well to try to mirror his example, model of love and generosity of heart. He is an author whose books have much to offer.

Jerold, my neighbor whom I previously mentioned in chapter two, who has an intellectual disability as well as mental illness, goes through a constant, daily struggle. I chatted with him about this one cool, sunny spring morning. I had just gone out back to take a bag to the dumpster when I saw Jerod approaching. I waved to him and then sat down on a stoop. He joined me, but sat down at a great distance.

"I'm so cold, I should have worn my jacket," he said.

I remarked that I was so fat I didn't need one.

He was wearing his usual outfit of sweatpants, tee-shirt, camouflage-design cap, and bright, white tennis shoes. He had a black money bag belt around his waist.

"How are you doing? I asked.

"Oh, all right. I usually say a short prayer to God in the morning; but when I'm really bummed out, I won't. I have a lot of problems."

23. "Jean Vanier," L'Arche USA, lines 1–28.
24. Ibid.

Jerold's face became distorted in obvious distress.

"Do you have enough food to eat?"

"I get paid today so I will have some food. And yesterday, I ate at The Catholic Worker House."

Just then he abruptly stuck out his feet in front of himself and asked, "Do you like my new shoes? I have diabetes so my insurance paid for them." He was very proud.

"Yes," I said. "They are very nice! So . . . you have a lot of problems?

"My brother put his dog to sleep. I really loved that dog; I walked it for twelve years. He bought another one, but I don't like it much."

I knew Jerold had just had a birthday.

"Did you have a nice birthday?" I asked.

His face brightened.

"Yes, my brother and his wife gave me lots of presents and twenty dollars!"

"How many siblings do you have?"

"I have two brothers and my sister died. She had epilepsy and manic-depression. She had a seizure and died."

"Oh, I'm sorry to hear that. What were your parents like? Was your mother a kind person?"

"Oh, yes!" Jerold glowed. "She smothered us with love! But my dad had a temper and used to beat my ass. I had a learning disability and had trouble in school; and when I was ten I had obsessive compulsive disorder but back then no one really understood what that was. And when I was twelve, I abused hard drugs."

"You mentioned Systems Unlimited before. What does that organization do for you?" I asked.

"They pay all my bills for me, using my income. I don't get food stamps, but I get a little housing assistance. I used to be able to pay my own bills, but I can't do it anymore. I also had a social worker but she dropped me."

"Why did she do that?" I asked.

"Oh, they said I said some things. I was on some sedatives and I couldn't control myself. I did some things over and over and I couldn't remember anything. I'm not on those drugs anymore." His face distorted again into obvious frustration and remorse. "I know how that is. My doctor had me on one called, Ambien," I said, "and I lost control of my behavior also. It ruined my ability to think straight. It was horrible. I know how you feel."

* * *

I will describe a model of psychiatric treatment that promotes recovery for someone with a severe or chronic mental illness and who needs long-term care. First, when there is a noticeable crisis or psychotic break, the person should be hospitalized in a psychiatric hospital unit or acute crisis center before transferred to a hospital. The patient will be allowed to stay as long as it takes to stabilize their condition, even if it takes one to two months or longer. If the patient lacks financial resources then psychiatric personnel, perhaps social workers, would see that the patient is started on either SSI or SSDI or both, as well as Medicaid or Medicare or both.

Next, upon discharge from the hospital, the patient can be placed in a psychiatric half-way house of about eight single-gender tenants where the patient can live for up to an entire year. Living in this type of group home can help prevent isolation and promote social skills learning. Here the person can do daily household chores and cooking. They can also apply for either paid employment or volunteer work out in the community after being evaluated by Vocational Rehabilitation or Goodwill Industries or both. Application of housing assistance would be vital and there would most likely be a lengthy wait period. Sometimes the person can attend college classes to help further their employment goals and improve brain function. Vocational Rehabilitation can sometimes fund this. If a person has religious leanings, they find a religious community of their choice and attend worship services, Bible studies and other gatherings.

Visits to the local mental health center's drop-in clubhouse for people who have a mental illness provides an opportunity to socialize, make friends, and improve work skills because the clubhouse is where clients can stop in to have a cup of coffee, chat with peers, and eventually, work on some projects. There can be group therapy led by a psychiatric counselor focusing on various topics which is also helpful in the recovery process.

Once a person leaves the half-way house and is living in their own home, usually an apartment, they can continue with volunteer work or employment and creating new friendships at the clubhouse. If the person is attending religious services, such a religious organization may have group meetings they can join and classes and eventually, a social network of support can be formed.

From the time of the half-way house the patient continues as an out-patient at either a community mental health center or a hospital clinic. The patient will need some kind of therapy to work through the trauma they have experienced, as well as any other long-term issues with perhaps a psychologist or a counselor, as well as to continue with their medication. Sometimes Cognitive Behavior Therapy (CBT) is offered which is to help with distorted thinking patterns. I believe that CBT has been initially created with good intentions, e.g., to correct unhealthy thought behavior patterns and to promote new, healthy ones. But there is a delicate balance here: a counselor attempts to correct the unhealthy patterns while at the same time is helping the patient to feel good about themselves and to not lose confidence in what positive abilities and qualities they have. If a therapist is going to constantly tear apart a patient's thinking, this will destroy any self-esteem the person has. A person needs to maintain a healthy self-image that not only recognizes their faults, weaknesses, and failures; there still needs to be an appreciation for all the good they can do (and think). As my advisor said to me: "There are many ways to go wrong; but also, many ways to go right!"[25]

---

25. Anonymous advisor, email message to author, January 10, 2018.

Chapter 5

He Stretched Out His Hand and Touched Him

> And a leper came to him, imploring him, and kneeling said to him, "If you will, you can make me clean." Moved with pity, he stretched out his hand and touched him and said to him, "I will; be clean." And immediately the leprosy left him, and he was made clean.
>
> MARK 1:40-42 (ESV)

ONE BRIGHT SUNNY MORNING, I saw Richard sitting on a stoop outside the Hills Bank. He looked quietly still, as usual, perhaps waiting for the bus. I thought his clothes looked rather dirty and his face more tan than earlier. He still had shoulder-length straight hair, only now wearing a cap, and continued to look very thin. I approached him, smiling.

"Hi, Richard, it is so good to see you! How are you—how've you been?"

He also smiled, greeted me, and said, "Oh, I'm fine, thank you."

I held out a dollar bill—"Here, this is for you; do you think you can use this?"

"Yes, I can," he said, "Thank you." And he took the bill.

"And I brought you something. But if you don't like this, you don't need to take it. Do you like this?"

I held out a bottle of Ocean Spray juice.

"It looks pretty good—I'll take it. Thank you."

"It's cold," I said.

"Oh, good. Thank you. I've been downtown since seven."

"Do you have an apartment now?" I asked.

Yes, I have a place now near Aero Rental. I share it with two others. We all get along. There are lots of dogs running around."

"I bet that gets kind of noisy," I said.

"I just roll over and go to sleep," Richard said with a chuckle.

"Does it have air conditioning?" I asked.

Even though it was spring we had had some ninety degree temperatures recently.

"Yes, it's cool," he said.

"What have you been doing lately?"

"Oh, paying bills."

"How long have you had your apartment?" I asked.

"Since the first of the year, the beginning of January."

"I'm very happy for you—that's answered prayer—I prayed for you!"

"Thank you, Marcia!" Richard said with emotion.

"Okay, bye now . . . I'll see ya."

* * *

My living conditions have improved since that cold winter in 1995. Temperatures can still fall below zero, but now my home is warm. I moved to the east side of town and occasionally the heating system has malfunctioned for a few hours, but the landlord promptly fixes it. I live in an area with multiple stores, banks, and a pharmacy within walking distance which is a great improvement, though now my body is slowing down and I am often in need of assistance to get groceries. I use a cane now to support my walking. The homeless in my city now have a warm shelter to stay in on cold winter nights. In addition, plans are in development for new affordable low-income housing units.[1] But this is just a drop

---

1. Gruber-Miller, "Shelter House," Iowa City Press Citizen, lines 40–44.

in the ocean; much more needs to be done. My current pleasant circumstances are not the norm—many are still out in the cold. As part of my ministry work I investigated the housing shortage in Iowa City. I wrote a report for the church committee under which I do my work. I told them the following concerning the low-rent affordable housing shortage crisis in Iowa City:

> I don't want to bore you with a detailed account of all my interviews and findings so I will make a summary here. I talked to people who work for the city, the University, and also at various centers and shelters. I also talked to the executive director of this region's Habitat for Humanity organization.
> The conclusion is that it would take many years of work to arrange funding and manpower to build or renovate affordable housing. However, The Johnson County Coalition for the Homeless has already secured funding for a program called *Housing First* or *FUSE*. This building will go up soon and house in about twelve units and without strings, the most chronic homeless—those with substance abuse disorders, and mental illness. But that leaves another 1,000 homeless who don't have anywhere to live and the many *working poor*, who work but can't find a place to live.
> I did not receive a warm welcome when I chatted on the phone with a director at the Housing Authority. He did answer my questions—though not in a very pleasant manner.
> The Homeless Outreach person at the Abbey Mental Health Center was very gracious—we met in person several times and had good discussions. Mark Patton, former Executive Director for Iowa Valley Habitat for Humanity, provided a lot of important information. He expressed willingness to construct housing for the low-income but said it would take many years to secure funding and other things such as man power, and resolutions of zoning issues, etc. And there would be nothing to stop the University students many of whom have wealthy parents supporting them, from taking such units for themselves so it would not reach the low-income general

public. Students would possibly cause a lot of problems, trashing the units because of parties, alcohol, etc. The director concluded with, "Capitalism will not help the low-income people; and because of this it is up to the government and churches to fill in—to help them."[2]

There is a big group of advocates for affordable housing in Johnson County who meet and hold events to problem solve. I elected not to join them. I am not joining any groups. The Iowa City Domestic Violence Shelter representative said her clients can only find housing in other cities, perhaps by moving to Cedar Rapids. She gave me a PDF file with a valuable slideshow of the FUSE program which was very helpful.

We need to ask, How did Jesus treat people who have disabilities? What do we see by his example? These two questions ought to be the focus for possible solutions to the plight of the mentally ill. With my advocacy, I hope to encourage others to promote within their congregations a warm welcome and an inclusive gesture toward those previously ignored or marginalized.

People with various intellectual, developmental, physical, emotional, and spiritual disabilities have for centuries been ostracized, neglected, and abused. Sadly, the church has often coalesced with the broader society by treating disabled people with scorn. Now, as many across our nation are fighting for the rights of those who have a mental illness, we, the people of God, have a duty to stand at the forefront in this justice movement. For, it *is* a matter of justice. Christ touched and healed the leper. Christ blessed and gave sight to the blind. He helped the mute to talk. He healed those sick with all kinds of diseases, showing loving compassion for all.

One of the goals I have is to encourage our congregations to create relationships of friendship with those previously ostracized because of their psychiatric disability; who've been previously rejected by the church and broader community. To accomplish these goals of a change in attitude and an increase in sensitivity, groups within congregations can creatively plan together and spur each other on in the implementation of educational actions through

---

2. Patton, email message to author, April 19, 2016.

displays, congregational social audits or surveys, church library resources, special worship services, and Sunday school and adult education offerings. Something I have implemented myself, is a mental health support and discussion group held in a central location in the surrounding community sponsored by the church. This is an ideal setting for inclusion and encouragement for people with mental illness themselves; families of those afflicted, and any others who have interest.

Mental illness reveals itself in more ways than the commonly held stereotype of radical examples of institutions—humans languishing without recovery, in miserable living conditions. Mental illness abides in people whom you see walking down the street, people holding down jobs, professionals, or non-professional, housewives, teens, or children in broken homes. Seniors are often afflicted with dementia in increasing numbers, unable to do self-care and who become dependent on family or specialty organizations.

People with mental illness are the most isolated human beings in the world. Once a person reveals their illness to their social group, this enacts shunning and avoidance. Former friends will not know what to say or they will be fearful and will back away from the person who revealed their illness. The mentally ill person may be pitied and condescended to. Stigma is a very great problem and that is one significant reason why those who have a mental illness are afraid to mention it to anyone.

Even though mental illness is a treatable condition, outsiders looking in have an attitude of rejection. A person can go into an emergency room at a hospital with a broken arm and there is no hesitancy on the part of health care workers to aid the person. However, when someone with a broken mental condition seeks aid, adequate treatments are often unavailable due to bed and personnel shortages; and there is little or no follow-up care. Public attitudes prevent resources from becoming sufficiently available to support the mentally ill population. Attitudes need to change.

Meanwhile, support groups can strengthen those afflicted with mental illness, their loved ones and friends. As I mentioned I began a Mental Health Initiatives support and discussion group in my community. I opened it up to anyone: those of any faith tradition or no faith. I wanted to provide a space where people can feel accepted for what they are—without fear of rejection—to bare their hearts either about themselves or someone they love. People have an enormous desire to share about their own lives or their loved ones' situations. Too much has been bottled up and for too long. On the first day of the sessions, participants of the group just spilled over in grief and frustration. Finally, someone would listen without passing judgement.

At the first meeting I asked the group the following questions and opened it up for discussion: *How is your situation—what do you need to talk about? What kind of challenges are you or your loved one dealing with personally? Are you able to access services? How has mental illness affected your or your loved one's life? How did it change your life? And, what has been the most helpful?*

As an example of how urgent the needs still are for the mentally ill in the twenty-first century I will share this real-life anecdote which occurred in the spring of 2018. I was just finishing my morning coffee around 4:30 a.m. in my living room as I read my devotional literature. My window was open to let in the cool, fresh air. Suddenly, I heard a loud commotion coming from the apartment complex next door, out in the parking lot. A young male voice was loudly wailing and bemoaning.

"I'm not lying! There was this white guy with long hair and a big Mexican. The Mexican pushed me. I went to her door and asked her for help. He pushed me. My head hurts real bad . . . ."

I got up from my chair and went to look out the window. In the darkness I made out a police squad car with its headlights shining on a young man sitting on the parking lot pavement. I made out a female figure dressed in black slacks and a bright red vest, and standing next to her, a male police officer in all black.

"Forget about it," the woman said loudly, bending over the young man.

"I don't want to forget. I'm not lying."

He held his hands on top of his head and said, "My head hurts," then repeated the same things over and over, loudly wailing about the white guy with the long hair, and the big Mexican who pushed him and that his head hurts.

"He's schizophrenic," said the woman to the male officer, as though that would sum everything up—no other explanation needed.

"Calm down, Curtis. Forget about it. Calm down," the woman demanded. "We are going to take you to the hospital."

But he continued wailing while she kept ordering him to calm down.

"I don't want to forget about it; I'm not lying. I went to her door to ask her for help and he pushed me . . . I don't want to forget about it. I'm not lying. I was assaulted. I landed really hard. My head hurts; my back hurts . . . ."

He cried out in desperation, pleading again and again.

Just then another police car pulled up and two officers got out. Then immediately following, an ambulance came. Two medics got out and approached Curtis; one did all the talking. He must have asked Curtis what was going on because Curtis, again, repeated the story in a desperate, distressed voice as though he felt no one believed him.

"I was assaulted—I landed really hard. I'm not lying. My back hurts. My knee hurts. My head hurts really bad. There was this white guy with really long hair and a big Mexican—he pushed me . . . ."

One of the medics asked him in a kind voice for his full name was and if he was allergic to anything. Curtis answered him and the medic went into the back of the ambulance only to emerge a couple of minutes later holding a syringe. Curtis was still wailing and pleading the whole time as the female continued to tell him to just calm down.

"Did you have something to drink?" the medic asked.

"I drank a half of . . . what are you doing?" asked Curtis.

"This is a sedative," the medic responded in a professional, courteous tone. "What is this on your arm?"

From my upstairs vantage point, I saw the medic injecting the medication and then they brought out a stretcher.

"Lay straight, Curtis," the medic said, still with a kind voice. "Lay on your back."

"My back hurts; my knee hurts. I landed really hard . . . ." Curtis kept repeating.

I saw Curtis lying on the stretcher and the straps pulled over his body and arms. He now seemed to be more subdued with only an occasional whimper. Silently, they put him in the ambulance and all the vehicles departed, bright lights oscillating.

My impressions are that it is a travesty for police or psychiatric personnel to say to a victim of assault, "Forget about it." To attribute a person's account of violence to only a fabricated, psychotic episode is cruel and inhumane. Even if Curtis really had schizophrenia and was in the middle of a psychotic break, it is still entirely possible for him to be, at the same time, a victim of a violent assault. The place where this event happened is in a high crime zone with drug lords, heavy alcohol abuse, and frequent sounds of gunshots. Homeless ex-cons are transient renters there or who just hang out at all hours of the day and night. It is a huge injustice to not sympathize with a victim of assault. Curtis's pleads for acknowledgment of his plight of very real physical and emotional pain went unanswered until a more compassionate voice sounded from the time of the medics' arrival. The medic who spoke had a more understanding tone of voice, showing some empathy, and maybe was possibly considering the truth of Curtis's story as they went about arranging his transport to the hospital.

It is important to give a person with mental illness the respect and dignity due to anyone who is in travail and distress. Victims of violent assault—considered being psychotic or not—need to be given every consideration for a healing treatment plan, both in short term hospitalization—acute care—and long term counseling or psychological therapy, to help them deal with the trauma they've experienced. Many people with mental illness are victims not only of assault from strangers, but are double-victims when their desperate cries go unheard.

A new development in my city to help this type of situation is a crisis intervention *access center*.³ This facility is to help divert people in crisis from jail and/or expensive stays in the ER. Police can bring a person who previously might have been jailed for getting into trouble with alcohol, drugs, or low-level crimes to this facility where they will be medically evaluated and placed either into psychiatric care or wherever they need to be. In the past, too many people with mental illness were arrested and incarcerated for minor offenses or just for being in an acute psychiatric condition that really just needed medical attention.⁴

This facility would include sobering and crisis stabilization, telemedicine, and a homeless shelter with few requirements for occupancy. Law enforcement officials are trained in substance abuse, homelessness, and mental health issues. Behavioral health specialists accompany police officers on calls to help evaluate a person in the acute situation and to direct their placement whether to a hospital ER or to a sobering and crisis stabilization unit. This effort is to keep people out of jails and expensive stays in the ER, and to get people the appropriate services and mental health treatment they need.⁵

When the mentally ill do find themselves incarcerated for low-level crimes or other more serious ones, it is possible they will lose all their financial support network that comes in SSI, SSDI, Medicaid, and Medicare, as well as their housing support. If a person is in jail for one month, their SSI will be halted. Then after they are released, they need to get their benefits reactivated. But if a person has a sentence twelve consecutive months or longer, they will have to re-apply and obtain approval for the benefits all over again.⁶

As you can imagine, a person would need assistance to deal with the paperwork involved; finding someone available to assist would be a stumbling block. Meanwhile, they have no shelter, little

---

3. Schmidt, Mitchell, "What's An Access Center?" The Gazette, lines 1–2
4. Ibid., lines 2–9.
5. Ibid., lines 11–18.
6. Psychiatric professional, email message to author, January 31, 2018.

food, or other needed support. Homelessness proliferates under such conditions, and with that, mental distress, crime—recidivisms—the revolving door. No wonder the emotional devastation is so great and subsequently, the need for Christian interventions with the aim to lift people out of this vicious cycle.

Psychiatry has yet to come to terms with the anger of the mentally ill. Bullying, abuse, and mistreatment at the hands of those in all areas of society builds a powerful anger in those mistreated—an anger that builds and builds to the point of explosion. Being unable to find an outlet for these extreme emotions causes a mental ill person to strike out in defense against family members, fellow students, and those in powerful positions of authority. When injustice is ignored and the vulnerable have no defense, a backlash of the greatest magnitude erupts.

If no one will listen to the person who has a mental illness; when people take advantage of the person's lowly position and refuse to acknowledge the concerns to the extent of cutting off further communications—then, why does a violent episode, emotional or physical, come as any surprise? Does the psychiatric profession expect docility and passivity from those who've been beaten down by the world, cast out from the mainstream, left to starve, to go without adequate clothing, and who are then left on the streets, homeless? When daily, the constant grind of one-down encounters emotionally club the mentally ill over the head, saying, *I am better than you—you, who are deficient, inferior, and less than human;* how, then, in any reasonable agreement, can psychiatry expect the mentally ill to remain silent? Why, is it any wonder that the mentally ill become upset, and more than upset, erupting into violent aggression and hateful words? If the psychiatric profession expects doormats of the ill, then they have failed their mission of defending those who've been placed in their care. If the psychiatric profession expects the ill to just take all the abuse and slander and remain silent to the detriment of their emotional health and well-being, then this profession is not only perpetuating the wrongs of society, but, in addition, it is reinforcing the injustices against mentally ill people who then have no recourse but to strike out and protest in whatever method they believe will give them a voice. Somehow, the mentally ill need to find a voice and be heard.

The answer to such outbursts is not to lock the mentally ill up behind bars of either the jail or psychiatric ward and throw away the key. The answer is to sit down and listen, and listen carefully, to what the mentally ill have to say. The mentally ill need someone in their corner, someone who will sympathize with not only their current situation, but with what has happened to them in the past that brought them to this place of anguish. The distraught person needs a nonjudgmental advocate who not only understands what the mentally ill are up against, but who will actively seek ways to provide for the needs for the ill. Food, clothing, shelter, humane treatment, loving relationships, meaningful work, joyful activities—all things denied must be reinstated in the full to reverse the downward plunge into the gutter. The affluent professional must step down from their ivory tower of comfort and ease to empathize with the rejected of society, those who have nothing at all, and whose anger has no place to be heard. Instead of cold indifference and accusations; the mentally ill need empathy and understanding—advocates.

Jesus Christ is described in various ways throughout scripture; in the Old Testament:

> He will rescue the poor when they cry to him; he will
> help the oppressed, who have no one to defend them.
>
> He feels pity for the weak and the needy,
> and he will rescue them.
>
> He will redeem them from oppression and violence,
> for their lives are precious to him. (Psalm 72:12-14 NLT)

We are asked to embody Christ on earth. A person cannot say they represent Christ and at the same time support oppressive laws and regulations that rob the poor and trample on the rights of the disabled. As noted in Matthew 6:24 (ESV), we either worship God or wealth: "No one can serve two masters, for either he will hate the one and love the other, or he will be devoted to the one and despise the other. You cannot serve God and money." Those who worship and serve God are going to reflect God's values of compassion and mercy.

Once I described how I want communities to treat the disabled and a friend replied: "Oh, you are describing the kingdom of heaven; you are asking for the kingdom of heaven."

Well, yes.

As we say in the Lord's Prayer: "Thy kingdom come, Thy will be done, in earth as it is in heaven." Matt. 6:10 (KJV) Left to its own devices, life on earth is hell and evidence of this abounds as we go about our daily lives in the fallen world. But as we look around there is also evidence of the kingdom of God. When we resist the urge to judge another person or when we do unto others as we would want done to us, this is a little bit of heaven. When we share what we have with someone less fortunate and strengthen those who've been beaten down, this is a little of the kingdom of heaven.

Tikkun olam is Hebrew for: *Acts of kindness performed to repair the world; ensuring a safeguard to those who may be at a disadvantage. Opposition to injustice.*[7] One of my ways I work to repair the world and oppose injustice is to give presentations to nursing staff and medical students at the University of Iowa Hospitals and Clinics, as well as a psychology department. I have been asked to share my story and what has been helpful in my recovery. Going back into my past over and over for the talks has been rather traumatic but I have done this to try to help others understand what some of the conditions are for developing a psychiatric illness, what it's like to be ill, and what factors help in the healing process.

In my previous book, *Voices in the Rain* (2010), I explained in depth the importance of religious faith combined with medication for the recovery process.[8] My intention in writing this memoir was to provide a counterpoint to Nancy Andreasen's *The Broken Brain*, (1985)[9] in which Andreasen, with tremendous over-simplicity and stark reductionism, left out the mind's great immaterial aspects and mysteries. Far from being a purely materialistic mechanism, I

---

7. Learning to Give; "Tikkun Olam," Lines 1–5.
8. Murphy, *Voices in the Rain*
9. Andreasen, *The Broken Brain*

maintain that the brain and subsequently, the mind, contain properties that lend themselves to supernatural dimensions. Though supernaturalism is difficult to prove empirically, it is even more impossible to disprove. And since it is impossible to disprove, science has no right to disavow. For science bases itself on facts, on what can be proven, and since supernaturalism cannot be disproved, the question remains open. Any bias against supernaturalism is purely prejudicial and opinionated, not factual.

In addition, as US psychiatrist, M. Scott Peck, explained in his work covering several decades: *Psychiatry will only succeed when it acknowledges and treats the spiritual dimension of mental illness.*[10]

Peck was a trailblazer who paid a heavy price. A look at his book that depicts his courageous encounter and confrontation with the demonic[11] shows his deep commitment to having been open to truth where ever that would lead him, even to the darkest depths and at the sacrifice of his own personal comfort, physical health, and peace.

Our country's materialistic culture with its pragmatic science contains whole segments of our population who live and work in denial of the spiritual or take it very lightly. Therefore, as a person who's experienced mental illness directly, and who has been a recipient of psychiatry services, I seriously recommend that modern psychiatry be open to follow Peck's lead who even as a medical scientist espoused a willingness to rediscover the spiritual origins of diverse manifestations of mental distress, origins uncomfortable for us to acknowledge, yet impossible to ignore.

As an illustration for the importance of spirituality in psychiatry, I will share the following.

Samuel, my downstairs neighbor who lives directly below me, is a tall, heavyset man in his late thirties who smokes. He has been emerged in a spiritual battle that I have witnessed. I know his name because once passing in the building hallway, we exchanged greetings, and I politely asked him about himself. He works in a warehouse, he said, operating a forklift.

10. Epstein, "M. Scott Peck," lines 100–123.
11. Peck, *Glimpses of the Devil*, xv.

Living in a low-income apartment building such as mine, tenants can hear each other doing things. I hear the neighbor at the lower-west side talking to his cat. I hear the neighbor on the south side swearing at people while on his phone. I hear the cat playing with rolling objects in the apartment directly next to me. And on my north, I hear my neighbor lady's radio. The walls, ceilings, and floors are of very thin wood so tenants hear each other going about their daily lives. And this is how I know that Samuel below me suffers from mental illness and severe spiritual distress.

The day he moved in, I became very angry with God. It was because Samuel would constantly walk around below me, day and night, going from one room to another, growling and snarling and speaking loudly in a low, deep, demonic voice—I had no idea whom he might be addressing. It seemed that God put this person here specifically to torment me, to disturb me by this devilish man. All my life I felt I had been surrounded by people who had bad behaviors, and now this. I was very upset with God. I lacked any kind of peace.

Not only did Samuel march around his home while speaking in the evil voice, he would violently bash objects around his apartment, flick his light switches on and off repeatedly (I could hear it); he slammed his windows open and then closed them so forcefully I thought the glass would break. He also slammed his door as he came and left his apartment. This went on for several years. He became especially riled on Easter holidays—they were especially distressing for him—and he made more noise than usual.

One early morning after an episode of this disruption, it seemed he became stationary, completely still in a corner of his room. I heard whimpering and moaning, sort of crying, whimpering and moaning. I pictured him lying in his bed, dejected and curled up. Utterly defeated.

I thought I needed to do something to intervene. So I went down and put a copy of my memoir, *Voices in the Rain*, outside his door.

Soon after, I saw the book on the floor by the mailboxes with a note on it: *Someone left this by my door by mistake*. I thought, how humble. I then put a note on the book: *This is for you, Samuel,* and once again placed it by his door. I knew Samuel was a reader because I had noticed him carrying bags of books in from his car.

Soon after I left my book, things began to change. I also enlisted my church's prayer ministry. I asked them to pray for Samuel, not only for his benefit, but that I might also find some peace. After I thought Samuel had time to read my book he seemed to calm down. With only a few setbacks, he stopped storming around. The demonic voice he spoke mostly abated. Once when running into Samuel while outdoors, he held the building's door open for me to enter. He looked very sad.

I asked him, "How are you, Samuel?"

He replied, "I'm tired."

What was in my book? I said that Jesus Christ is the answer to mental illness along with medication. I said that Christ has defeated the demonic powers and that a person needs to put their faith in him to be restored. Christ is Lord and our salvation. I told the story of my life which involved near-destruction of my being and how I slowly climbed out of the hell that tormented me. Maybe it gave Samuel hope and a seed of faith. I certainly hope so.

I ask that psychiatric professionals give Dr. Peck's work an opportunity for teaching us about the unseen realm where battles in the mentally ill often take place. Peck was a man of science but who also kept an open mind. His work should not be ignored.

What I see as a serious problem is the modern-day fifteen-minute *med check*, what the current psychiatric appointments are called. Often patients are not provided the courtesy of discussing their concerns at length. This is a travesty. When patients do not have a chance to discuss problems as in *talk therapy*, the patient is dismally deprived of any help. Medications administered without verbal *give and take* to discuss psychiatric problems in depth is close to no help at all.

Fortunately, most of my providers over the years have stretched the fifteen minute rule to include longer sessions which included psychotherapy. But this is an exception rather than the rule. Upon intake, in general hospitals when the patient is first interviewed, a brief psychiatric history is taken. However, this is not enough. I would like psychiatry to go back to the traditional weekly, hour-long, in-depth interview sessions that were provided for me when I was first placed under psychiatric care. My psychiatrist allowed adequate time to go over my past in detail and also addressed my present urgent needs which were difficult to deal with. This early care provided the emotional support I would otherwise not have been given elsewhere.

Patients' traumatic injuries and mental breakdowns which are a result of a long history of familial or societal abuse and mistreatment cannot be solved within a brief, fifteen minute med check. The ludicrous notion that patients' deep-seated psychic ills are curable with a quick fix of a pill has got to be corrected with real talk sessions with a healthcare provider that will continue on indefinitely with the aim of uncovering layer upon layer of emotional and mental maladies. Yes, medication can, and often does, provide some relief; but medication, alone, has been and remains, inadequate for deep and sustained healing. Only with the direct human compassion experienced in therapeutic give and take of talking and being heard, can one sort out the immense complexities inherent in mental disorders—disorders that were more often than not built up over the course of patients' entire lives through innumerable social interactions and a myriad of events.

Some clinics have a minimal number of providers available to do talk therapies as well as insurance issues that prohibit a large number of psychiatric patients from obtaining care. Because of the shortage in psychiatric professionals the wait list for psychotherapy is long, leaving patients to languish in their struggles unaided. This lack of providers is a serious, complex issue that cannot be solved overnight. We need compassionate people entering the field that have confidence that they can make a difference and who are in it for the long haul. Providers face many challenges: long hours, heavy patient load, and acquiring the self-care necessary when dealing with tragic, horrible issues which take their toll on a provider's own personal mental and emotional health. Healthcare professionals need their own support network to bolster their work and when this is lacking lives can crumble.

Psychiatric healthcare providers, whatever their own backgrounds, bring unique talents and abilities to the field. A helping hand can come from anyone or from surprising places: I am a firm believer that God can and will use anyone or anything God chooses to accomplish his purposes. This includes people of any faith tradition or even a non-believer, rich or poor, sophisticated and educated or simple-minded, young or old, and of any race or ethnicity. My view of God's power and sovereignty is without limits; I don't put God in a box. Wherever there is a willing heart to extend a compassionate hand to help others less privileged than themselves, God is there, and often God will use the examples of *outsiders* or *those not in the social club*—the hated—to prove a point, put us to shame, and teach us the right way to live and act. And once in a while an authentic Christian witness will come to the fore carrying the message of Christ's love for the downtrodden—taking seriously Christ's message to serve.

One example of such a Christian witness to help the poor and mentally ill can be found in a fellow member of my religious community. Though her organization cannot provide long-term psychotherapy (and is not a model for psychiatric care), it still addresses some of the basic physical needs that psychiatric patients face when coming to her for assistance.

I asked Cecilia Norris, MD, medical director of the Free Medical Clinic, to describe her work and what the clinic provides for those who have little or no health insurance. The clinic's clientele are all low-income; many who have psychiatric problems seek medical care for their over-all general health that leads them to this clinic.

The objective in describing this clinic and how it operates is to show an exemplary model that can be duplicated elsewhere. A non-profit organization, it opened in 1971 and is the second longest running clinic of its kind in the United States after the Haight Ashbury Free Clinic in San Francisco which opened its doors in

1967.¹² Dr. Norris says, "I think that health care should be a right and that we all have a responsibility to help those in need however our talents allow us to. I am fortunate to be able to do this in an environment that is inclusive, understanding and committed to give patients the best health care we can."¹³

The following is a list of questions I asked Dr. Norris with her responses:

1. Do people with psychiatric problems come to your clinic for psychiatric treatment?

    Yes, but we are unable to provide ongoing psychiatric services or ongoing counseling. If patients have minor psychiatric disorders that can be managed by medication checks and visits every three months, I can prescribe some medications to help with those problems. We do not prescribe any controlled substances or medications that require very close monitoring.

2. What do you do for them? What are most outcomes?

    It is variable. I see a lot of patients with Post Traumatic Stress Disorder and it is very difficult to treat that without a team approach of psychiatrist, psychologists, group therapy. Some patients with mild depression and anxiety do well.

3. Are there substance abuse issues?

    Yes. We refer patients to Prelude but it is frequently difficult for them to accept that they need help.

4. Is there a predominance of certain types of disorders/diseases that your clinic sees?

    Mostly diabetes, high blood pressure, thyroid diseases, asthma, acute conditions such as urinary tract infections, sinus infections and sexually transmitted infections

5. What are the various financial situations of your patrons?

---

12. Norris, email message to author, January 17, April 10, 2018
13. Ibid.

Most are at the poverty line or below. Some make too much to qualify for Medicaid but cannot afford individual insurance. Over fifty percent of our patients work.

6. What kind of situations and concerns does the dentistry clinic see?

   Dental hygiene clinics for cleanings, fillings and certain extractions (not molars or wisdom teeth).

7. Do people get prescriptions for medications at the clinic?

   Yes, they either get prescriptions or the actual medications themselves if we have samples or supplies to give them. We try to get patients on chronic medications enrolled in patient assistance programs through the pharmaceutical companies so that patients can get expensive medications for free if they qualify.

8. What kind of follow up do the patients get, if any?

   In chronic clinics, we typically see patients every three to six months depending on how well controlled they are. If they have an acute problem that requires follow up with a primary care provider, we are usually able to do that. We have some specialty follow up available but not a lot.

9. How long is the usual wait to see a medical person once they have made the appointment?

   For acute problems less than a week, chronic two to three months.

10. What community agencies help a person make an appointment, if any?

    Mobile medical clinic, hospital social workers.

11. If a person has a life-threatening condition what are their options?

    Emergency room.

12. If they need continual treatment, what are their options?

    Depends on the condition: if it can be controlled with medications and life-style changes we can see them at the Free Medical Clinic. If they require specialized testing or surgery, they need to work with social workers at the hospitals. Unfortunately it is very difficult for a patient to be able to get surgery in this city if they don't have insurance and it is not emergent.

13. How often are you willing to see a single patient?

    No limit as long as they are not abusing the appointments and we have them available. If patients need to be seen more frequently than every one to two weeks, we cannot usually do that. Over what span of time period? Some patients have been coming to the FMC for over twenty years.

14. If a patient cannot pay anything, do you still see them?

    Yes.

15. What if they cannot afford medication?

    If we have medication samples we can give them, we try to give them those. There are several medications on the $4 plans at area pharmacies so we will frequently look for some of these that we can substitute for medications patients are on. If it is a one-time need for a medication—for example, an expensive antibiotic—we have a voucher program. A patient can get one voucher for a prescription for up to $50 once a year.

16. How many physicians work in the clinic?

    Two part time paid, fifty volunteers. What kind of shifts do they have? Three to eight hours a day. Some volunteer weekly, others once every few months. I work twenty hours a week and the other paid physician works ten hours a week.

17. How do you acquire physicians and staff?

Mostly word of mouth for physicians. When we are short on volunteers, I try to speak to medical associations. We advertise for other staff and most other volunteers are by word of mouth or someone who knows someone who works at the clinic.

18. How do you get your funding?

    In general: United Way, Johnson County (Iowa), Cities of Iowa City and Coralville, private donations, in-kind services. Some small grants for specific programs or equipment.

19. Is this a constant annual challenge?

    Yes. The way we are structured, we have to cut services if funding is short.

20. What counties do you serve? Or can they come from anywhere at all and be treated?

    Anywhere.

21. What is the predominating atmosphere or attitudes you encounter from the surrounding communities, what do people (general public) feel about your clinic?

    I think most people realize that the clinic serves a very important role in the community. More and more hard-working as well as disabled individuals are unable to obtain insurance. Most people I have talked to have expressed gratitude that the clinic is here and pride that our community can offer this.

22. Are there some difficulties with prejudice toward the clinic and the population you serve?

    Yes, but I do not think it is just because people use the clinic. I think prejudice is against the underlying reason for people needing to use our clinic—mental illness, poverty, minority populations, and immigrants.

23. And if so, how is this expressed, and what can be done about it?

    I hear more about how employers take advantage of workers and racist things said to patients by others in the community. I think what can be done about it is something that I do not have the expertise to address.

24. How supportive are the religious communities in our area of your clinic?

    Very.

25. What are your concerns about the difficulties the clinic may currently be experiencing (political, economic, etc.) and what are your hopes for the future concerning the clinic?

    I am more concerned about the difficulties that patients of our clinic may be facing than the difficulties of the clinic itself. The FMDC has enjoyed strong support from our community, especially when it has been needed more. My true hope is that we will no longer need the FMDC and that we will have universal health care for all. In this current political climate, especially, I do not see that happening. I strongly oppose health care being run as a business because this neglects the innate "value" of all people and reduces health care to a commodity that can be sold only to those who can afford it. With the economics of our time, the rich are getting richer and the poor and middle class are working harder just to stay where they are. I think it is telling the average pay of health insurance CEO's in 2015 was 28.5 million dollars and the median was 17.2 million dollars. This at a time when our country has worse health outcomes than twelve other developed countries with some form of universal health coverage. The US has the highest infant mortality rate and lowest life expectancy of these countries.[14]

---

14. Ibid.

He Stretched Out His Hand and Touched Him

Once a basic foundation of economic survival is established I see recovery the following way: It is not necessarily the absence of all symptoms. It is when a level of stability is reached. People can take part in meaningful activities; form and maintain significant relationships; make a contribution to society; and do ones best with life's challenges. In recovery, mental illness does not define the person—identity comes from positive sources.

Recovery from mental illness can be defined as the point when a person takes a step beyond mere coping to find meaning and purpose in their life. It is when a person sets out to see what they can accomplish, what they are capable of.[15] It is when their lives are enriched by learning and expanded beyond any societal-imposed limitations. A person needs a positive outlook with a good attitude, as well as the support and guidance of psychiatric professionals, religious and civic leaders, and mentors.

There needs to be meaningful work to do. "Work that you love is a great gift, something to be thankful for. Most people don't have it, and one goal of good social policy is to create more jobs that are actually worth doing."[16] People with mental health challenges also need access to education with time to find and discover inspirational resources. And they need opportunities to express their creativity and playfulness.

In the twentieth and twenty-first centuries many people who have a psychiatric condition may have had or currently do have more education and access to technology which will enable them to broadcast in various media what is happening in their lives, their struggles, and challenges. It is now, more than ever, possible for conditions to be exposed and there are ways to inform the public about bad situations and has the potential to be a great catalyst for change. Over the centuries, a recurring theme throughout reform efforts has been the importance of education: spreading helpful information throughout every strata of society has been, and will continue to be, paramount to influence minds and hearts.

15. Clinebell, *Basic Types*, 29.
16. Anonymous advisor, email message to author, January 10, 2018

God calls his *people* his treasure: "The LORD has declared today that you are his people, his own special treasure" (Deut 26:18). And in Matthew 18, Jesus speaks of God the Father giving special attention to the needs of "little ones" (18:10). The phrase refers to children, but it also includes everyone who might be categorized as one of the "least of these" (Matt 25:40). The chronically ill, disabled, mentally ill, all those who are unable to care for themselves or provide for their own needs—God especially treasures these.[17]

On more than one occasion I have wepted over the plight of the mentally ill. One time, as I was giving a presentation for medical students—something I've done for many years on a regular basis—at the point of giving the statistics on how many of the homeless are mentally ill, I broke down crying and had to stop for a few moments to gather my composure. Eventually, I did keep speaking and forwarding the slides.

And when preparing a mailing distribution of some ministry materials, a CD with a PowerPoint slideshow on how the church can help the mentally ill, I prayed as I worked, my heart filled with a longing for the fruitfulness of this project. Would anyone respond to this great need? Would anyone care? Who would be God's helping hand?

> Never walk away from someone who deserves help; your hand is *God's* hand for that person.
>
> Prov 3:27a (MSG)

It all starts with a helping hand. You can be that person who makes all the difference in someone's life. I am very grateful for the kind and compassionate psychiatric professionals who have aided me over the years. Without them, I never would have made it. I am grateful to the institutions and leaders: members of the church, physicians, educators, and librarians. There are many who have stood in the breach. *And I sought for a man among them*

---

17. Beyond Suffering Bible, "Guarding God's Holy Treasure," 545.

HE STRETCHED OUT HIS HAND AND TOUCHED HIM

who should build up the wall and stand in the breach. . . . (Ezekiel 22:30a ESV)

> "Standing in the breach may take different forms in different times, but standing in the breach always involves placing yourself between evil and those who are innocent. Standing in the breach always involves injecting yourself into a dangerous equation, so as to effect a good and just outcome. Standing in the breach is always a form of taking up the cross of Jesus to protect those who are defenseless. Standing in the breach is standing up for those who cannot stand up for themselves."[18]

Reinhold Niebuhr, one of the greatest thinkers of the twentieth century, spoke of the great modern pessimism in perspectives on the state of humanity. He expressed the futility in trying to excuse the vast depravity within man. Yet, he also said that man has a great capacity for justice and it is the duty of a people to work for change and to not give up hope. Niebuhr is a man who witnessed both World Wars during his lifetime whereby prohibiting him from any trace of naïveté. Yet, when someone expressed the futility in attempting to improve the human condition, he still encouraged action and positive thought in the cause of justice. As a Christian theologian and philosopher, his point was that even in the face of evil humans must work for the good and never give up hope.[19] I, personally, would challenge anyone who states that *things never improve*. History has proven this otherwise as we see in women's suffrage, civil rights and even medical care.

Not only do we need advocates for the mentally ill who have the responsibility to aid and support those who are struggling; but those who suffer from mental illness have a responsibility as well. For Jesus said: *I am the light of the world. Whoever follows me will never walk in darkness, but will have the light of life.* (John 8:12 NIV). We must turn away from a destructive lifestyle, seek healing and renewal from a higher power, and heed the wise

---

18. Grant, "Standing in the Breach," Bon Air Presbyterian Church, lines 42–43.
19. Robertson, *Love and Justice*.

counseling of those who've been given to us to help lead us out of darkness. *How often I have longed to gather your children together, as a hen gathers her chicks under her wings, and you were not willing.* (Luke 13:34 NIV)

When I first started doing research for this book, my grief and distress over the history of the conditions for the mentally ill and psychiatric methods for treating those with mental illness was so profound that I was completely devastated and so I had to put the project aside for several years. As I recovered from this initial attempt, I gathered strength in numerous ways: I gained new and broader social support from my church; I gained more strength in additional reading; I found healing in the waters of a swimming pool; and I worked on additional projects which bolstered me emotionally. And I prayed. I prayed for courage and strength, not only for me but for my doctors, religious community and leaders.

I say, *Hats off*, to the many psychiatric professionals who've sacrificed their own comfort and countless hours to work in the clinics often without one *Thank you*. I remember during one spring break just one, solitary psychiatric doctor manned the outpatient clinic, seeing dozens of patients all by himself, all week. Many psychiatrists have come and gone, some burnt out from the endless tragedies shared by patients in the telling of their stories. Heroic social workers, psychiatric nurses, and even the clerks at check-in: they all play a part. Who can be seen? What medications will be administered? Where else can the patients be referred, to what services and supports?

But most of all we need to ask: what are the patients' stories? How did they fall ill in the first place and how did they enter into a psychiatric system to where a battle for resources and commodities is a desperate daily struggle? Why did they suffer so emotionally and so completely become broken vessels that survival has become nearly impossible? Where are the families and what have they been doing to help, if at all? Where are the friends, neighbors, and civic organizations?

The answers to these questions will be key to finding a solution not only for psychiatric disorder, but will heal a broken system in the care, support and treatment of the mentally ill. The individual and societal problems inherent in mental distress need a complete cultural response. Political, religious, educational, and medical answers to mental illness must first of all be grounded in compassion and nonjudgmentalism.

Who are we to say who deserves help and who does not? How are we any different than a person who is mentally disabled? Are not our own disabilities often hidden but yet just as profound? Aren't our own weaknesses as significant as someone else's? A bit of introspection will alert us to the fact that we, too, have reliance on others, a dependence interwoven so complex it is mind-boggling. No human can make it on their own and any such assertion is self-deception. And then, it is in such humility that people will acknowledge the responsibility to help others whose needs are blatantly obvious: those sleeping under a bridge; in the meal line at the Free Lunch; standing at the door of the Crisis Center Food Pantry. It is in such humility that a young person in medical school chooses to specialize in psychiatry. It is in such humility that the social worker elects to go into the field of counseling.

Because without acknowledging our own shortcomings, we will continue to look down on others and see them as *less than*. I don't know what it will take to change this centuries-old crisis we are in. Often, it takes having a family member who is ill to wake us up. But even then, this is often not enough. I know as someone who has experienced the devastation inherent in mental illness myself, that at one point I would have committed suicide without the gracious and courageous efforts by psychiatric personnel. In fact, I almost died once by my own hand, but was revived by doctors in the ER. I don't know the religious backgrounds or personal perspectives of all these people, strangers to me. But I do know they had a reverence for life and sought to keep me going for whatever purpose God ordained. By their efforts I am still alive today.

I will close this narrative in the only way possible; that is to say a prayer and leave it all in God's hands. My prayer is that homes can be schools for teaching values of treating others respectfully, and with a reverence for life—life for those of various races, ethnicities, cultures, and different ways of being a part of this world. I pray for compassion to fill the hearts of those who currently have hard, uncompromising hearts. I pray for a reallocation of resources and for government officials and civic organizations to have the wisdom to do this fairly. I pray for educational institutions, that teachers, professors, and students can appreciate their privileges in being allowed the time and place to study schools of thought supporting human rights. And I pray for the development of a fair and just social order.

Most of all I pray for the church, that it will stand in the breach. That it will take a stand when justice is denied the innocent, that the church will defend those whom countless times have been silenced; to move to include those once despised and rejected. The church must spearhead the movement of responding to the cries of the mentally ill as it has done so many times in the past however insufficiently, and now seek to make lasting, powerful, and substantial change. To do so, I pray that the church will model, uphold, and create a substantial new reality stemming from the vital mandate taught by Christ: *A new commandment I give to you, that you love one another: just as I have loved you, you also are to love one another.* (John 13: 34 ESV)

In Jesus Christ's name I pray,
Amen and Amen.

Bibliography

American College of Rheumatology. "What is Fibromyalgia?" accessed May 24, 2018. https://www.rheumatology.org/I-Am-A/Patient-Caregiver/Diseases-Conditions/Fibromyalgia.

Bainton, Roland H. *Here I Stand: A Life of Martin Luther.* New York: Penguin, 1977.

Beyond Suffering Bible. "Guarding God's Holy Treasure." New Living Translation, 2016.

Borba, Michele, *Building Moral Intelligence: The Seven Essential Virtues That Teach Kids to do the Right Thing.* San Francisco: Jossey-Bass, 2001.

Cary, Phillip. *Augustine: Philosopher and Saint.* Teaching Company Great Courses (Audio), 1997.

Clancy, John, "In Memorandum: Paul E. Huston, MD, PhD, 1903" Annals of Clinical Psychiatry vol 1 (1989) issue 1 5; Published online: 12/04/2011, accessed on 4/03//2018. https://www.tandfonline.com/doi/abs/10.3109/10401238909149857.

Clinebell Jr, Howard J. *Basic Types of Pastoral Care and Counseling.* Nashville: Abingdon, 1984.

———. *Counseling for Spiritually Empowered Wholeness: A Hope-Centered Approach.* Binghamton: Haworth Pastoral, 1995.

———. "Mental Health Through Christian Community." *Pastoral Psychology* 20, no. 5 (1969) 34.

Davis and Bunting, "The Poor Farm Matter," The Evening Gazette, July 28, 1887, accessed June 2, 2018. NewspaperArchive.com.

Encyclopaedia Britannica. "Catholic Worker Movement," accessed April 19, 2018. https://www.britannica.com/event/Catholic-Worker-Movement.

Epstein, Robert. "M. Scott Peck: Wrestling With God." November 1, 2002, last reviewed June 9, 2016, accessed May 2, 2018. https://www.psychologytoday.com/us/articles/200211/m-scott-peck-wrestling-god.

Farraj, Myrna. "Hope," In *More God, Less Psychiatric Illness: Devotions for Those in Recovery From Mental Illness,* Marcia A. Murphy, ed. Cedar Rapids: Eagle Book Bindery, 2017.

The Free Dictionary. "Transpersonal Psychology," accessed May 26, 2018. https://medical-dictionary.thefreedictionary.com/transpersonal+psychology.

Bibliography

Gollaher, David L. *Voice for the Mad: The Life of Dorothea Dix*. New York: Free Press, 1995.

Goodman, Barak. *The Lobotomist*, DVD, Directed by Barak Goodman and John Maggio. PBS Home Video; 2008.

Grant, R. Charles. "Standing in the Breach," (sermon), Bon Air Presbyterian Church, November 16, 2008, accessed April 10, 2018. http://bonairpc.org/Sermons/Sermons%200708/sermon16nov2008.htm.

Gruber-Miller, Stephen. "Shelter House Lines Up Location for Emergency Winter Homeless Shelter." Press-Citizen. Nov. 13, 2017, accessed April 16, 2018. https://shelterhouseiowa.org/news/shelter-house-lines-location-emergency-winter-homeless-shelter/.

Hanson, Brad. "Trial Must Be Moved." KWWL, updated October 10, 2017, accessed March 24, 2018. http://www.kwwl.com/story/36558468/2017/10/Tuesday/trial-must-be-moved-for-dubuque-man-accused-of-2015-sexual-assault-killing.

Huston, Paul E. "The Iowa State Psychopathic Hospital." *Palimpsest* 54, no. 6 (November–December 1973): 11–27; 55, no.1 (January–February 1974): 18–30.

Johnson County Historical Society. "Johnson County Historic Poor Farm," accessed October 9, 2017. https://johnsoncountyhistory.org/poor-farm/.

Kaiser, David. *How the Hippies Saved Physics: Science, Counterculture, and the Quantum Revival*. New York: W.W. Norton & Company, 2011.

L'Arche USA. "Jean Vanier," accessed April 19, 2018. https://www.larcheusa.org/who-we-are/jean-vanier/.

Learning to Give. "Tikkun Olam," accessed March 24, 2018. https://www.learningtogive.org/resources/tikkun-olam.

Lee, Kevin, "Iowa's Winter Cold Temperature History," Sciencing, updated April 25, 2017, accessed October 13, 2017. https://sciencing.com/iowas-winter-cold-temperature-history-7443044.html.

Luhrmann, T.M. and Jocelyn Marrow, eds., *Our Most Troubling Madness: Case Studies in Schizophrenia Across Cultures*. Oakland: University of California Press, 2016.

McCarty, Jean. Interview with author, January 12, 2001.

Miltner, Mr. and Mrs. Joe. National Register of Historic Places, First Johnson County Asylum, Iowa City, Johnson County, Iowa, National Register #781001226. Iowa State Historic Preservation Office in Des Moines, Iowa, and the National Park Service in Washington D.C.

Mostert, Mark P. "Useless Eaters: Disability As Genocidal Marker In Nazi Germany." *The Journal of Special Education* 36 no. 3 (2002) 155.

Murphy, Marcia A. *Voices in the Rain: Meaning in Psychosis*. Cedar Rapids: Eagle Book Bindery, 2010.

NAMI National Alliance on Mental Illness. "About NAMI: Who We Are," accessed May 24, 2018. https://www.nami.org/About-NAMI.

BIBLIOGRAPHY

National Archives, America's Historical Documents. "Thirteenth Amendment to the U.S. Constitution: Abolition of Slavery," accessed April 11, 2018. https://www.archives.gov/historical-docs/13th-amendment.

Peck, M. Scott. *Glimpses of the Devil: A Psychiatrist's Personal Accounts of Possession, Exorcism, and Redemption*. New York: Free Press, 2005.

Philadelphia State Hospital (Byberry). Opacity, accessed April 24, 2018. https://opacity.us/site10_philadelphia_state_hospital_byberry.htm.

Pietikainen, Petteri, *Madness: A History*. Abingdon: Routledge, 2015

Reinders, Hans. *The Future of the Disabled in Liberal Society: An Ethical Analysis*. Notre Dame: University of Notre Dame Press, 2000.

Rickers, Terry. "Mental Health in Iowa: Lack of Facilities Makes Task Difficult." Des Moines Sunday Register, July 31, 2011.

Robertson, D.B., ed. *Love and Justice: Selections from the Shorter Writings of Reinhold Niebuhr*. Philadelphia: Westminster, 1957.

Schmidt, Mitchell. "What's An Access Center?" The Gazette. Feb. 14, 2018, accessed on February 28, 2018. http://www.thegazette.com/subject/news/government/whats-an-access-center-20180214.

Systems Unlimited. "About Us," accessed April 19, 2018. http://www.sui.org/.

Watkins, C. S. "A Necessary Institution." The Daily Gazette, April 20, 1873, accessed June 9, 2018.

Wikipedia. "Psychological Abuse," accessed April 13, 2018. https://en.wikipedia.org/wiki/Psychological_abuse.

Wright Jr., Frank L., *Out of Sight, Out of Mind*. Preface, para. 1. Disability History Museum. Courtesy of Swarthmore College Peace Collection. http://www.disabilitymuseum.org/dhm/lib/detail.html?id=1754&page=all.

www.ingramcontent.com/pod-product-compliance
Lightning Source LLC
Chambersburg PA
CBHW071440160426
43195CB00013B/1984